My Year on The Road

My Year on The Road

How The Tubbs Fire Sent Us To Europe And The Camp Fire Brought Us Home

Kim McGrath

Copyright © 2020 by Kim McGrath

All rights reserved. No part of this book may be reproduced or used in any form without the written permission of the author except for the use of brief quotations in a book review.

Printed in the United States of America

First Printing, 2020

ISBN 978-1-7355449-0-8

Cover design and interior text layout by Leo Baquero, leo_baquero@hotmail.com, www.LayoutAdaptationDesign.com

Preface

At dusk on Saturday October 8, 2017 my husband, Bob, a former California Department of Forestry worker, said, "Get some stuff, our papers and emergency things, by the door. I don't like this." This being the hot wind that had just picked up and tossed our garden umbrella onto the hill.

I did. Insurance papers and a few odds and ends because, of course, what he was thinking would never happen. This was when I realized that my earthquake preparedness kit was a shelter-in-place kit, not something to toss in the back of the car and leave with. A Go! bag is a different creature.

He went to bed about 10:30 but was back up soon after.

"Something's wrong."

"What?"

"I don't know."

He left in his truck to drive our little neighborhood and found fire two streets up from us on Sullivan Way. It had started the way many California wildfires start. High winds knocked down a Pacific Gas & Electric power line into a tree. Sparks ignited the dry grass underneath and then the tree. Fire trucks did respond because at that time there were trucks available. Four crews arrived and they included my husband in their efforts once he told them he was former CDF. Then a call came and all but one of the crews took off. The final crew pulled equipment and told Bob he could stay on with the hoses. They didn't have time to wrap them up because something big was coming.

The house uphill from the downed PG&E line was demolished. The neighbor's house then caught and was gone, too. Over the next ten days the swimming pool of the original burn site would be the water source from which my husband and a friend would ferry water to hot spots that needed dousing.

The two houses across the street from the downed PG&E line did not burn. The fire came into the yard of one, but no further. The wind was blowing southeast, up the hill and away from them. Had it started later in the night, when all the engines were involved in the Tubbs fire, or if the wind direction had shifted, the fire story for Santa Rosa would have been different. Spring Lake and Howarth Park were next in line.

As it was, Bob stayed the night at the fire scene and at a vantage point on that road for viewing the fire coming over the hills from Napa. I tried to go to bed, thinking of how little I had put in the Go! bag. I got up several times to look out the windows and add things to the bag. The wind was blowing hard, branches were cracking and dropping. I considered moving to the family room couch to avoid the branches of the oak tree outside our bedroom window. About 2:00 a.m. a friend called.

"Are you being evacuated?"

"No. You?"

"Yes."

"Come here."

They did. More than 4,500 people evacuated from Oakmont, a planned community with only two access streets to Highway 12. Our friends had been awakened by an oak branch falling on their roof. They went outside to see the damage, saw the fire, saw the cars driving down the road, and listened to their neighbor when she said everyone needed to get out.

When they arrived around 3:00 a.m. the fire had been plainly visible from our driveway for some time. Spots of red advancing forward towards us, and sideways towards each other. The wind kept blowing as it does in the fall sometimes, like a giant wind tunnel has been switched on, bringing a fire like no other since 1964.

For the ten days Oakmont was evacuated we four plus three dogs stayed in our house, Bob and our friend venturing out into the neighborhood for regular checks on homes and people while putting out the hot spots at the top of the hill in the first burn site. Some older residents didn't want to leave, so he kept checking in with them. Other people had left in such a panic that they left doors open and lights on. Carefully, and

I do not recommend this to anyone ever, he called out to see if anyone was home, then entered to be sure there wasn't someone in need, then turned off lights and locked the doors behind him as he left.

My friend and I ventured out to the store a few days into the situation. The sky full of smoke, but cars on the roads, stores open, banks open, Montgomery Village in operation, mail being delivered. It was hard to put the fact of the destruction of the fire next to the fact of life going on.

We were in between two evacuation zones, never ordered to evacuate, except for an accidental evacuation order. A Sheriff's car from central California went through the neighborhood giving the evacuation order via its speaker system. We were outside talking with a neighbor who had returned to see how the neighborhood was doing. The sky was windless and surprisingly clear. It turned out the evacuation order was a recommended evacuation on the other side of Highway 12. Oops. Many people rushed away after that, not knowing the mistake.

Technology helped satisfy the need to know what was going on. Nixle alerts, signing on to So Co Alerts, and signing up for Santa Rosa Police emails kept us informed. Plus using flightradar24 we were able to sit on our couch and watch digital helicopters fly over our house to scoop water out of Spring Lake and head off to the fire while listening to the whump whump of the real helicopters as they passed over.

I met a Cal Fire officer at the gas station one evening while I was adding a few gallons just to be safe. He was on the phone while washing his windshield. I caught his eye and gave him a thumbs up and mouthed "Thank you."

He said, "Mom, I've got to go. There's someone I need to talk to."

Then he asked me if I had a place to go. I looked back at my car full of boxes, like I might be homeless. I assured him I did, my home was safe for now, but I was ready to go if needed. He asked where I lived, then drew me a map that showed where the fires were, where they were expected to go next, and assured me I was perfectly safe. This, he said, was the latest news as he had just come from a meeting of the commanders. This he told me because I had told him that our son, still in the US Virgin Islands doing relief work after being stuck on Puerto Rico during Hurricane Maria, was more than worried, was in fact frantic that we get out.

"Tell him what I told you. Tell him you'll be fine."

In the end we were and so were our friends. The $400 worth of newly purchased groceries in their fridge and freezer were not as PG&E had cut the power to Oakmont. But both of us had our homes, our pets, our stuff, and each other.

We also had sub-clinical symptoms of Acute Stress Disorder. When Bob and I left the house to go to a meeting for survivors all I could think about was the fact that we had left my son's two King Charles Cavaliers at home alone, and what would happen if there was another fire? Not many people had yet returned to the neighborhood. Who would rescue them? It was easier to turn around and go home when the traffic turned out to be so snarled that we would have been late to the meeting. Sniffing the air, looking out the window to check the sky but not to see the view, obsessing about keeping the car tank at least half full, obsessing about cell phones being charged, keeping the television on tuned to local news, and not sleeping because somebody had to be awake. These abated over time for us. Not for others, especially those whose loved ones, houses, or businesses burned in the firestorm.

But life goes on. Appointments made before the fire came up and what reason was there to cancel? 'I'm afraid to leave home' wasn't acceptable to us. We didn't want to get stuck in that fearful place.

So Bob went to his appointment at Kaiser Medical and while checking out got to talking to the department head. Bob told him that before the fire we had been working toward selling our house and moving, so if any of the more than two hundred doctors and staff at Kaiser who had been burned out were looking to buy they could call us.

Within hours we were getting calls from doctors and staff wanting to rent. We did not want to be landlords. We wanted to sell. Dr J and Ms S were smart enough to have their insurance company call with an offer for an obscene amount of rent money for twelve months, to which husband said, "You know it's only a three bed, two bath house, right?" They offered more. We took it.

And this is how we came to find ourselves on the road for a year.

Our plans for retirement have been to remain eternally young. That hasn't worked out. We have a very small 401k and a valuable home. For several years we toyed with various plans revolving around selling and moving. Husband took early retirement and in the spring I had closed my therapy practice in anticipation of marketing our home and leaving.

Where to move was always the problem. Two exploratory trips to Portugal, and several years learning the language made it seem plausible. Now with rent money feeding into our savings account every month we could try living there and other places on our list as well. We combined our desire to see if we could live abroad with some volunteer work. With a list of seven locations in Portugal, Ireland, and Germany we began to plan. Not well and with lots of mistakes, but we planned.

We had already sold a number of our things before the fire. Now with the lease signed the push was on to pare everything down to the minimum. Move out day was one month away. We sold, gave away, hauled to the thrift store, and tossed the accumulation of four decades together. It is a hard process. While it frees you up, it also wears you down. Each item carries its own emotional weight. Continually carrying that weight as you delve into the memories and decide whether to keep, toss, or give away is a workout for your heart.

At last, down to four suitcases that would travel with us through one year and four seasons, the stuff we cared about enough to pay to store went into a 10x15 unit and didn't fill half of it. Or it didn't until we came back over and over to put back things we'd removed from our suitcases and drag boxes around to get to things we had decided we did need after all. Traveling light, or light-ish, is hard work.

Then we left for Oregon. We spent a week on our own in a cabin by a creek with the rain pattering down, gathering strength, visiting gardens and waterfalls and a Frank Lloyd Wright house. We ate German food and found lots of former Californians to talk to. Then on to visit family and friends we hadn't seen in years and visiting family who had themselves packed up and moved away from California. This was both a time to try out our ability to live small, and a post-retirement catch up. Finally we boarded a plane to Portugal.

As landlords renting our own home, we had fewer worries. When something malfunctioned, we ourselves could call the warranty company we'd hired. But getting an email from our tenant whose subject line is

"Burst pipe" shaved a few days off our lifespans. It turned out to be an irrigation pipe which he had already repaired.

It seemed we had made the ideal deal. We were getting an exorbitant amount of money each month for rent and we were going to live cheap, banking lots of cash for our retirement years. Except that the rule of life is pretty much the same as the rule about remodeling your house: everything will cost twice what you thought and take twice as long.

"Traveling is a brutality. It forces you to trust strangers and to lose sight of all that familiar comfort of home and friends."

Cesare Pavese, 1949, Italian novelist

Portugal

Here's some travel advice for free. Make your reservations well in advance. Make a plan. Go ahead. Spontaneity isn't all it's cracked up to be. Spontaneity is great for folks who don't mind sleeping in a hostel dorm with snoring strangers. For those who like quiet and order, plan ahead. This also helps in car rental. Rates go up the closer you get to the pickup date. Ordering from the US is best. Our dilemma was that we wanted to keep some freedom. We wanted to be able to say that we were done with this spot in Portugal and were ready to move on. Or to be able to take advantage of the flash sale on air fare to Denmark, say. Reality crunches that naivete. Best rates in vacation homes are for long term stays. Best rates for a car are given the further away your pickup date is. It's crazy in a way. Imagine if you had to book a table at a restaurant a month ahead to be sure the prices would be reasonable. Who would do that? Oh wait, I just found a restaurant reservation system that does just that – books you two months out. I still ask, "Why?"

When you arrive in a country (let's just leave off discussing the insanity of air travel and air reservations. Charging for a seat? Charging for blanket and pillow on an overnight flight? Charging for earbuds so you can hear the "free entertainment"?) and you want to get to the place you've rented, hoping it looks something like the lovely pictures posted by the landlord, you will sign at whatever price they gouge you with. It's the nature of travel. Exhausted, cranky, sore, miserably dragging those ridiculous suitcases over another curb is more than you can think of. Give me the car! And they know it, those lovely people back at corporate. They've got you. You should have ordered a car months ago.

If you're able to handle the bus ride with transfers to get to the hostel dorm, go for it. If you're only going for a week, stuff your backpack and go forth boldly via bus or train. If you're with me, and you've got two suitcases, be glad we have reservations.

The houses we rented were more than I would like. But that's not because of timing, but because my husband is like a big cat. He likes the country. He needs his space. (See the Claymation *"Creature Comforts"*) Therefore, we need a house and we need a car. A room down the hall in someone's apartment near the center of town is like a prison sentence for him. A bumpy dirt lane to a house set amongst trees and tall grass is freedom for him. Horta das Oliveiras in Boliquieme was our new temporary home in the Algarve.

On that dirt lane we found what looked to us to be a Dutchman's Pipe vine wrapping itself around one of the trees. In Sonoma County it is a rare plant, one that attracts the Pipevine Swallowtail butterfly, also rare. The German neighbor at the end of the lane came driving by as we were snapping pictures and asked what we were looking at. When we showed it to him, he said, "Oh, that stuff. It grows all over the gate and I have to rip it off all the time." For a moment we could say nothing as we remembered how we baby our single vine and wait for the butterflies and then the larvae. It was only one of the many lessons on perspective we would learn during our year on the road.

About a week into our Portugal adventure we had been out walking. Tired after a couple of hours of up and down hills on dirt roads we stopped at Aldi supermarket for something to make for dinner. Spanish tortillas, more like a scalloped potato dish, became a freezer staple from Aldi's. This day down the first aisle I came across a familiar label: Trader Joe's. There was a box of peanut butter and another of dried cranberries. I snapped pictures and swallowed back tears of relief. It was to be a familiar feeling in the months ahead. While enjoying the bounty of our year on the road finding something from home felt like unexpectedly finding yourself face to face with a friend you haven't seen in too long.

A few weeks amongst the orange and tangerine groves with permission to sample the sweet fruit, wandering in the peaceful sunshine of southern Portugal's Algarve was a dream respite. Except for the unexpected raging thunderstorm which turned our dirt lane into a creek. This didn't seem too much of a problem because the sandy soil lets water drain away quickly. The problem with the rain came up the next day when our water began running golden. The cistern feeding water to our little country house had been inundated. Very fine sand came through the shower head and into the sinks.

Husband went online and found a townhouse that was going to be ready May 1. The owner agreed, after checking with his housekeeper, to let it to us early. Saying goodbye to the little house in the orange groves was hard. The move from country to the suburbs was bearable for husband because it would only be for a couple of weeks.

One thing that was easier in the townhouse was that we had an actual address. To get to the little house in the middle of the orange and tangerine groves we were told to Google Lick, the local nightclub, and wait in their parking lot for the owner to meet us. Then we drove down the road to a dirt lane and then to the third house on that lane. Our address was a GPS coordinate. Using MapsMe (an app that along with WhatsApp seems to be in use everywhere we went) we could navigate the way home from our adventures with no problem. To tell someone how to get to our house we texted the coordinates. In the townhouse we had a more familiar style address: a street name and an alphanumeric combo. In some neighborhoods we saw houses with two different numbers. Locals told us it was a project to simplify things like mail delivery. In the interim certain areas had two addresses, which didn't seem simpler.

Money

Euronet ATMs worked best for us. Before we left the US, we went to our bank where Maryanne and Symon were a great help in getting us set up with a credit card that has great travel benefits. We increased the amount we could withdraw from ATMs, making it easier to get the cash we would need to pay rent. Even with increased limits on our end, some ATMs have their own limits on what they allow for withdrawal. In our year on the road we did not have security issues with any ATMs but favored Euronet because we could get our max withdrawal allowance. Our only glitch was that my ATM card would renew while we were on the road. Sister-in-law came through again and mailed the card to us when it arrived. Mary Anne and Symon weren't happy about the potential security issues, but USPS and Irish Post came through and it arrived without a hitch while we were in Ireland.

Our first ATM in Boliquieme, and the best one, was at the BP service station across from the nightclub Lick and what would become one of our favorite restaurants, Ratatouille. Six-hundred euros with no fee.

Laundry

At home if I needed to wash something for the next day, I just threw a load in the washer, then in the dryer and went to bed. Here laundry takes planning. The washing machines I've dealt with are difficult to figure out. Our first had a book with a poorly translated English section. The others didn't have a book of instructions and their dials were a mystery of numbers, letters, and symbols. The first load at the Albufeira townhouse took more than two hours. We went to lunch, did errands, came home and it was still running. For load number two I turned the dial to a random number and symbol, and it took about an hour, which is an improvement. Once a load is done you have to have sufficient daylight left to dry it all. If I put a load in as soon as I get up, let it take it's time washing, then put it out on the line it will probably be dry by dinner. Maybe sooner if it's warm. But not always. So several times we've brought the drying rack inside or laid damp laundry on the backs of chairs, over the back of the couch, on hangers on a curtain rod. Laundry requires planning.

Which has changed my view of what's dirty. No more tossing whatever I wore today into the laundry. Check it out. Any spots? How big? Can I get that out with a little hand washing? Sniff test. Just like a bachelor! This is what a clothesline has brought me to.

It has also made me realize that my neighbors in Portugal know more about us than our friends do. Neighbors know if it's boxers or briefs, grannies or thongs, pajamas or nighties, and just what kind of sheets we have. These are things I don't know if anyone outside of the two of us ever knew until I had to find a sunny spot to put the drying rack. And I know these things about my neighbors too, even if our conversations are limited to my child-like Portuguese. And I'll tell you this: No thongs in our neighborhood.

Dogs

Dogs are, for the most part, working animals. Their job is to guard property, which they do, some with a frightening amount of sincerity. Many dogs live outside. We know this because we hear them barking in the night. No cushy spot at the foot of the master's bed for them. They're outside guarding in the night. Some wander the streets. We're told they're abandoned. They look pretty good for abandoned dogs. And they're neither aggressive, afraid, or interested in coming over for a scratch. They're independent and self-sufficient. Unlike my son's lovely Blenheim Cavalier girls who are chipped and recorded and wear identity tags, these dogs are on their own, but not lost.

Which brings up another interesting quirk. It's hard to find a house that is not behind a gate. Walls are the norm. Folks don't seem to mind driving up to their home, hopping out of the car, opening the gate, getting back in the car, driving in, getting out of the car, closing the gate, all the while making sure the guard dog is still inside the fence or wall.

In our first house in the citrus groves the owner arrived to drop something off for us and found that we had left the gate open. She was equally horrified and concerned. She assured us that while we were perfectly safe it made no sense to leave the gates open for anyone to enter for who knows what purpose. Following her advice led me to be found one morning by the orchard workers in my pjs, camera in hand, banging on the 8-foot metal gate to get my husband's attention. No bell. The gentle breeze had been enough to close the gate behind me, leaving me outside without a key. It had been a lovely post-sunrise sky and I got some great pictures, and the men who muffled polite laughter perhaps enjoy telling the story from their point of view.

Plaster walls abound. Metal shutters lock over doors and windows. Bars over windows. But people tell us we're perfectly safe. It's a wonderful country, No worries. Then why the gates? And bars? And walls? The gypsies, they say. Yes, they're here. If you're on the road and see a horse pulling a wagon, it's a gypsy holding the reins. And we're told they will steal anything that's not anchored in cement. We don't have the experience to know what's true and what's myth. But that's a lot of plaster, cement, shutters, and gates for folks in wagons. According to my Google research the crime rate in Portugal isn't any worse than anywhere else in the EU. The murder rate is so much lower than the US that it's shocking. More people are murdered in your average US city than in the entire country of Portugal. Perhaps it's the walls, gates, and shutters. Maybe we should follow their example. If they can't get to us, then they can't murder us. Still, it's hard to reconcile the security measures with the assurance "It's perfectly safe here!"

Limestone and basalt blocks roughly, and the rough is literal, from about one-inch square to four inches square are what make up many of the sidewalks here. They're lovely black and white reminders of Portugal's past. Interesting patterns are made from them both on the sidewalks and in the plazas and squares all over Portugal. They are also treacherous. Soil subsidence allows the blocks to rise or sink leaving ringed depressions. Toe-stubbing, heel catching, foot-slipping treachery is what they cause. You must really pay attention. No strolling along while looking up at the sky. A daydreaming stroll could land you in the hospital. Much of the Algarve where we are now is on sandy soil, so laying smooth cement sidewalks presents a true challenge. I appreciated those there were for the ability to stroll along admiring the sky and the landscape and the sea without taking a tumble.

Heating

The bikini-clad folks of both genders frolicking in the Atlantic waves and baking on the sunny beaches that you have seen in pictures of the Algarve only do that in the warm months. And when beach frolicking weather isn't happening it can be cold. In the townhouse we moved to after the country house there wasn't even a little space heater to plug in and move from room to room. We went to Oriente Perfeito (rough translation: Perfect Orient), an emporium of Chinese products, to buy a space heater with an unstable balancing foot and an amazing output of heat. We propped it up against a chair and tucked a rock on its foot to keep it balanced. Then we worried about the chair spontaneously combusting from the blazing heat the tiny heater produced. We moved it to the corner fireplace hearth (wood burning – no wood provided). And that is the only heat source for a two-story, two-bedroom, two-bath townhouse, and only because we bought it. My theory is that the constant struggle to keep warm, to be always bundled up, never quite comfortable, makes people anxious and worried, leading to gates, and walls. Though we will not be here to see the flip side of this, I theorize that the lack of air conditioning in the heat of a semi-tropical summer will do the same. Of course, I am a spoiled Californian accustomed to both central heat and air and to ocean breezes in our wine country valley. So maybe I don't have the right perspective.

Plumbing

A curious dichotomy for me is the presence of bidets and the lack of electrical outlets. My first thought at the lack of outlets was that electrical work is expensive, so limiting the number of outlets lowers the construction cost. But plumbing is also expensive, and the bidet not only takes up valuable floor space, but costs money to purchase and install. In the second place we rented the bidet was right next to the shower with a hand-held shower head. I am the lost American.

Electrical

A lesson we could learn from Portugal is cement electric poles. In California we put up wooden poles soaked in creosote, hang electrical lines on them and then wonder at how fast fires start. First in Boliquieme and then everywhere I paid attention many of the poles were cement. Down our dirt lane in the middle of the citrus groves and the tall grass the poles were all cement. I'm sure they have downsides, but fire isn't one of them.

The limited number of electrical outlets makes for interesting cooking. In the Albufeira townhouse there are two outlets at opposite ends of the kitchen. One is by the door next to the built-in drain board, meaning there isn't anywhere to put an electric kettle or toaster. So the single outlet at the other end of the kitchen was for the kettle, the toaster, and the microwave. If we wanted toast and tea, we had to make one first, unplug, plug the next appliance in, and proceed. Either our toast was cold or our tea was cold.

In Ireland we would find that you need to check the little switch on the wall plug. We thought an entire house was without electricity until one of us clicked the little switch and there was light.

I am realizing how spoiled I am for conveniences. I'm hoping that one of the benefits of staying long-term in various European homes is that I'll become more flexible, less judgmental, freer, lighter, more accepting. I'll settle for being really appreciative when we go home.

Driving

After we got used to the placement of freeway signs we were fine. It's when you get off the highway and into a town that things fall apart. It's like we're at war and people have torn down the road signs to thwart the enemy. What did people do before Google maps or Maps Me? Either of these apps will tell you to turn on say, Rua Independencia, but there's no street sign on Rua Independencia. And if, as happens frequently, the app isn't quite keeping up with your actual progress, then the order to turn comes after you have passed the turning. Then, and here's why roundabouts are good, you go down to the next roundabout and come back at it again, forewarned this time. It's a good thing we have unlimited mileage with our rental car. And it's a good thing there are two of us: one to drive and one to look at the screen checking for the unsigned turnings.

Food

Our first landlord gave us a list of restaurants we shouldn't miss while we're here. Mato a Vista in Paderne, was worth the hunt. We had a real time finding it because we hadn't yet learned that some highways, by which I mean numbered roads, look like alleyways or driveways. We pulled into what we thought was a driveway hoping to stop a moment and give the map app a chance to catch up. Then we realized it wasn't a driveway, but the road, one lane at this point, that we were looking for. After running between houses for the equivalent of a couple of blocks it widened into a two lane dirt road and except for a few brief patches of asphalt it stayed a dirt road until we turned a curve and there was the restaurant where linen tablecloths, excellent wine, and delicious food in a deluxe setting awaited us. It's a wedding venue as well. We were joined at our meal by a tortoise escaping the wet conditions of the night before. Wherever he'd been he was mud-covered and eager for a respite from the damp. The restaurant owner returned him to his spot beside the well where we found him later sunning himself.

We returned many times to Ratatouille because it was just around the corner from our house in the orange groves and because it was delicious. The daily menu is written on a giant chalkboard. Multiple tables are set and waiting for the lunch crowd of local working folk. Nine to twelve euros gets you your choice of meat – always meat – cooked in a multiple of ways, along with potatoes, and the usual salad of lettuce, tomato, and onion. The wines on offer are good and inexpensive. Your choice of dessert and a coffee is included. The coffee served in a tiny cup with a bag or two of sugar is sippable jet fuel.

Meat is a major component of the restaurant offerings here, and it has always been good. Turkey, called peru, is tasty but unrecognizable. Butchers here work to a different cutting chart. Chicken, very tasty chicken, is cut up into pieces which I recognize as wing and thigh, but the breast doesn't look like any chicken breast I know. Sometimes I don't recognize the cut-up bits as any known portion of a chicken, but the meat is chicken and it is delicious. Piri-piri, a delicious peppery sauce that is not hot in the same way Tabasco is, does amazing things to simple chicken. Mushroom sauce is always good and reminiscent of stroganoff but when it's on a chunk of chicken with piri-piri it becomes something differently delicious.

Pork is big also. And delicious. Yes, there's a theme here. The food in Portugal is wonderful. Sometimes as expensive as California, but sometimes so cheap we wonder how they're able to do it.

Husband is the fish eater and has a great time eating octopus, dorado, scabbard, and fish whose names we don't recognize. It's all fresh, flavorful, well prepared and makes him hum with delight. The scabbard is an Atlantic specialty with enormous teeth and huge eyes. It looks like a black eel trying to be a fish, and according to husband is sweetly wonderful. Stuffed with shrimp and accompanied by a cheese sauce husband says it's amazing.

Finnish friends who live in the Algarve autumn through spring and then go back to Finland for the summer took us to Portimão for the lighthouse view. We were to see on Madeira what we saw that day, an interesting cliff formation studded with what might have been bubbling pools that solidified mid-bubble. We walked around two giant holes in the cliff top that led straight down to surging ocean. They were larger versions of Hawaii's blowholes, and we don't know if water actually comes back up through them because we weren't there at high tide. A low fence around them did not keep husband from stepping over to see the precipitous drop. What we did see was a tour boat approach the cliff below the lighthouse. It came perilously close by way of what we could see from the cliff top. Then it disappeared. Turns out there are caves in the cliff big enough for these boats to cruise into. If there are pirate stories to go with the caves, we didn't hear any.

That same evening, after a late afternoon coffee and pastry, we drove to Carvoeiro, a beach you have probably seen when looking at pictures of the Algarve, selected to feature because it's a beautiful classic bay, festooned with colorful boats, and plenty of restaurants lining the street leading down to the beach.

We got a bit of Africa next morning when we went out to the car and found it covered in a fine reddish-brown silt. Friends called it Sahara rain. A Sahara sandstorm mixes with an Algarve rainstorm and you have Sahara rain. We respectfully fingered up some of it and had a look at African dirt, reminded again how far from home we were.

The Algarve reminds us of Southern California mixed with a little bit of Mexico. The weather and the terrain are similar. Since we had been here in a previous hot August we planned to be out of the Algarve before summer heated up too much.

As departure day loomed we knew we'd seen less of southern Portugal than we imagined we would. A train ride to Tavira never happened, and Tavira is worth visiting as we knew from an earlier trip. A sight-seeing venture to Silves for architectural sights was abandoned because of the crowds. Names of places we did visit roll off the tongue: Loulé, Almancil, São Brás, Vilamoura, Porches, Portimão, Querença, and Purgatorio where the apple pie was very good. We were filled with memories of the places we had been to, the friends we made, and the challenges we overcame.

Several European trips taught me how hard travel can be, and how rewarding, and fed the idea that someday I would be off with a bag and a list of places I wanted to see. Now I am in Portugal with two bags and a list of places we want to go. And I'm sometimes near being overwhelmed by the anxiety of not knowing where I'm going next, of not having things reserved, certain, assured. Having a home provides a security that masks anxiety. For me long-term travel keeps fueling that separation anxiety. There is no place to which I return and refuel. In one way this feels good because challenging the anxiety is one way to defeat it. In another way it feels like panic lurks at every schedule change, at each transition.

Husband has his own issues. When he feels his anxiety about crowds head towards panic, he will walk away from the scene. Yet he seems, to me, strangely unconcerned that we are without firm plans for the summer, which only fuels my anxiety. "Let me drive," I say, as if that would calm his anxiety any more than mine when he says, "Don't worry. It will all work out."

My only worry, because I didn't know better, about our upcoming flight to Madeira was that husband and I had both gotten sick about a week after arriving in the Algarve. I acquired a middle ear infection which was treated handily by a doctor at the International Health Center in Albufeira. Fifty euros for the first visit, thirty for any subsequent. Husband went in with me because his cough gave no signs of going away. The Doctor took us in together – no HIPAA here. We didn't sign any paperwork, no release or promises to mediate instead of sue. There was no COW (computer on wheels), just a 5x7 index card for both of us on which the doctor made her notes. We weren't weighed, nor was our blood pressure taken. I always question why doctors are surprised that my blood pressure is elevated when they have the nurse take it after they've weighed me but before I find out if I'm going to get jabbed, or sliced, or sent somewhere for a test. Of course it's up. I'm on alert. At home my bp is fine. To do without the check was a nice surprise, especially since my ear was throbbing, I felt like I was on a rocking boat, and everything sounded like I was underwater.

We took the piece of note paper with the doctor's stamp to a pharmacist where we got four prescriptions for 24 euros. A 20-pill package of 500 mg paracetamol (Tylenol) was one euro. Our prescriptions were all in blister packs, not bottles. You can't spill them, and they're easy to count.

I went back to the doctor about ten days before we were due to fly because I was still mostly deaf in the right ear. She took a look and told me that if I was a pilot I would be grounded, but I would be able to fly as long as I took a pain pill before the flight and was prepared for some pain. That is why pilots are grounded, she said, the pain on landing is too distracting. That put the blood pressure up.

After two months in the Algarve we depart for a month in Funchal, on Madeira.

Madeira

The flight goes well. There was discomfort, but no screaming pain. My seatmate didn't even know I was working my lymphatic massage techniques. (Google 'Lymphatic massage for middle ear infection.' It did help.)

A flight from Faro to Lisbon, a night at an airport hotel, then a morning flight to Funchal Airport where our new landlord, João, meets us to take us to our temporary home, a sea view house. Our ride was a fast introduction into the unique experience of island driving.

Madeira, closer to Africa than Portugal, sometimes called the Pearl of the Atlantic, is beautiful. A volcanic island thrusting out of the bluest ocean into the sky. Remember that volcanic and thrusting bit. The driving here is insane. We are staying in an old neighborhood, though we are not in the designated Zona Velha (Old Zone). The road we hike up to from our front door hosts a bus in one direction or the other about every half hour. The road is wide enough for a car. It is a two-way street. I'm not making myself clear. Buses run both ways on a curving single lane road with blind curves. The road down to our house is incredibly steep. So when we prepare to leave I ask husband, "Road of death, or hill of death?"

Our driveway is so steep that a stairway is set in the middle to make walking up and down easier. When we jokingly ask about parking in the carport by the house, João shakes his head, surprised. "No," he says, "it's not an easy driveway." We agree. Getting down it in a vehicle would be an adventure, potentially landing you another story down in the backyard. Getting up it would require a masterful hand on the gear shift and someone holding the gate open up on the street and stopping traffic because there would be no pausing at the top, and no way to see what was coming anyway. You would come out like a car in a San Francisco chase scene flying over the hills. And could you brake in time to keep from hitting the inevitable parked car across from the gate? It's an adventure we do not undertake.

Some locals honk as they come to a blind corner, but they don't slow down. The honk is a warning for whoever is coming to back off. A local said we would become 'habituated' to the driving if we stayed long enough. Driving fast and tailgating is the norm and works just fine once you're used to it. We have not seen many cars with evidence of a crash, but then the cliffs are so steep that perhaps they just push them over and let them drop.

While husband doesn't like roundabouts – he tends to take the first exit without knowing which exit he wants – they do allow a return without going around the block. Going around the block in Funchal can mean going down and left and left again and then right and then along the waterfront and then through the tunnel and now you can try again. This island has been lived in for many centuries, long before population and vehicles made a grid the logical choice for setting up a city. (Christopher Columbus in his pre-1492 days married a local woman and lived here for a few years.) And how would a grid be set up on the steep slopes of this lovely island? You have to follow the terrain. And you have to respect the ingenuity and engineering skills of those who have terraced the hillsides for roads, homes, and bananas. We look up valleys, amazed to see houses affixed to hills so steep we wouldn't consider them useful for anything except the occasional deer or mountain goat. But there are the houses and the terraced gardens and the roads to get to them. The bananas, small and intensely flavored, growing in all those terraces are sold across Europe.

Our first morning on Madeira I decided I needed a walk. Perhaps the thrill of the ride the night before with João had made me too giddy to realize how steep and how far a walk up to the main road would be. I did it. Just the once, because once is enough.

What I found at the top of the hill just above a small park with a view to the harbor where the cruise ships dock was Zarco's. This sea view restaurant was to be a regular stop for us. The espetada was some of the best and the friendly staff a source of much information and help with the language. Returning home I had to snap a picture of the handicapped parking spot near one of the bus stops, facing downhill on the steep slope. We never saw a car parked in it. Can't imagine a walker much less a wheelchair on that incline.

We arrived on Madeira at the tail end of the annual Madeira Flower Festival. We missed the parade but the decorations were everywhere and an abundance of flowers. Tents on the waterfront show off the local bounty in the form of amazing bouquets and displays. Everywhere we saw the fecundity of the island. Hydrangeas were blooming pink and blue, and agapanthus (lily of the Nile) has naturalized and flowers alongside roads all over the island.

We took a drive up into the mountains to Curral das Freiras, or Nuns Valley. It's a hiking jump off spot. And it would be easy to jump off. Too easy. Hold onto the sidewalk railing, please. It was significantly cooler with amazing views that reminded me of the Alps. Though smaller, these mountains are intensely steep. There was no gradual building up of the land. Explosive, convulsive land-making happened here. And then the Portuguese came and made a village. The road up was steep, winding, but wider than town roads. Buses had more room to make the hairpin turns.

Caves are everywhere on Madeira. Those near roads are sometimes turned into picnic spots, complete with fire pits and tables. On our way back down from Curral das Freiras we stopped at one where a family was grilling meat and sausages as water splashed down beside the fireplace. Grandparents, parents, and children cooking in the cave with water to splash in.

The Madeiran bus drivers must be amongst the world's best. They come at speed through narrow streets, leaving only inches between themselves and cars, walls or pedestrians, never flinching and, according to locals, rarely making a mistake. The only bus crash we heard of happened after we left and involved a tour bus, not a city bus. We looked for, but never found, a scratch or a dent on a city bus.

The pilots also deserve a mention because if you Google Funchal, Madeira airport you'll see pictures that had I seen before we decided to come here would have made me say, "No. Not going." Before they built the airport, people arrived by seaplane. There isn't enough flat land to make a runway, so eventually they built a runway out from a cliff over the ocean, like a gigantic freeway overpass to nowhere. On the freeway headed to the airport you drive under the runway among the enormous columns, then up and alongside the runway. My departure video shows the cars driving alongside of us as we taxi out for takeoff. If the pilot is off by even the slightest bit, you're in the ocean. If the brakes aren't fully operational, or the engines not cooperative, you're in the ocean. If the wind is blowing a bit too hard, you're in the ocean. A local told us not to worry. "We're only the fourth most dangerous airport in the world. We were five, but number four closed." I don't know if that's true, but from the day we made our reservations I began getting regular notices that the Madeira airport was closed for the day. Storms were coming in and making landing impossible. Sometimes planes get as far as the island and it's determined to be unsafe to land. Either they turn around and go back to Lisbon, or they head for Porto Santo, a small neighboring island with an inland runway. People are put up for the night and then ferried over to Funchal the next day. Pilots who are licensed to fly to Madeira and the Madeiran bus drivers are in their own class of brave and eminently capable.

We actually checked with a travel agency to see if we could get off the island on a ship. No dice. You must arrive on a cruise ship to be able to leave on one.

In the meantime we can eat. Espetada is a specialty of Madeira. This is beef, chicken, pork, or a combo of these on a skewer. Your choice of meat is cooked quickly in what looks like a pizza oven. The skewer is brought to you and hung from a hanger in the center of the table. With knife and fork you slide the meat down the skewer and on to the waiting plate. Piri-piri sauce straight out of the bottle is hot, but when chicken is cooked piri-piri style it's just flavorful and deliciously spicy, not jalapeño hot. Piri-piri is often provided tableside for those who like the burn. We couldn't find a bad meal anywhere we went. And we went lots of places. Quintinha do Churrasco offered us something we had been searching for: a daily plate for a low price. From noon to four for six euros you get chicken, salad, fries, and rice. Excellent deal. Excellent food. It was one of the places we returned to and brought friends to.

In the downtown tourist zone are many good restaurants. Many of these have folks standing outside to offer you immediate seating, enticing you by telling you the specials of the day. One day as we were headed back to the parking garage (lots of space, inexpensive and right next to the Funchal Cable Car at the edge of the Zona Velha with a Euronet ATM just across the street from the auto entrance) husband was enticed at Marisqueira Tropical by the offer of barnacles, something he has never tried. The waiter offered him a sample. He accepted and in minutes was handed a plate of barnacles to try while standing on the sidewalk. The waiter joined in to show him how it's done. Then he gave us a card with an offer of free wine with our meal. At another restaurant we were given a 10% off card for a return visit. A few days later we went back to Marisqueira Tropical for lunch. No barnacles that day. Husband had octopus risotto and I had chicken with mushrooms, both excellent. We got to talking to the man at the table next to us, a former corporate lawyer who had turned to the tourism business, running tours on Madeira and in Lisbon. Here is where we found out about the EU and Portugal.

When Portugal joined the EU in the 1980s funding was provided for infrastructure. Madeira has an amazing system of freeway and tunnels. The longest tunnel we were in is 2,400 meters (1.51 miles). One of the tunnels has both an off-ramp and an on-ramp inside. We will be taking the off-ramp just to be able to say that we took an off-ramp in a tunnel. A waiter at another restaurant (yes, we're eating out a lot – such good food) borrowed a book from a nearby store to show us how it used to be. The narrow one lane, two-way street we are staying on was the norm for many of the roads. Getting to Ribeira Brava was a three to four-hour journey from Funchal along roads like the one outside our door. Now it is about 15 minutes via a four-lane freeway (Via Rapida) and several tunnels. EU money was well spent on the road infrastructure. Without it I can't imagine 200,000 people could function in Funchal.

The Jardim Botanical, accessible via bus, cable car, and car, is rightly one of the things for which Funchal is famous. One way or round-trip tickets are available for the cable car. You can ride up to Monte from the easy to find Old Town location on the waterfront, take the brief walk to the second cable car that takes you down to the Botanical Gardens. Then walk down through the 20 acres of gardens spread over the hillside and catch a bus into town. Or you can walk back up through the gardens and take the cable car back down. We opted for the round trip to challenge my fear of heights and go via cable car, as if the airport wasn't enough. Oh oh oh oh! Steep hills and deep canyons make for amazing views. I kept my eyes open almost the whole time. Husband was well behaved and didn't rock the car. The presence of other passengers kept him in line. Up one cable line, then a walk to another cable car and back down to the Botanical Garden. Husband backed out after the second garden level saying it was too steep for him. By the time I was at the bottom of the garden I had to decide if it was better to walk back up to find husband, or just to walk on down to the center of Funchal. We had paid for round trip, so back up the mountain I went, glad of the chance to see again all the beautiful semi-tropical and tropical plants, pools, waterfalls, grottos, ferns, vegetables, trees, native plants, beds of plants laid out in geometric patterns, formal gardens, topiary, a recreation of a native thatch roof house, and a house converted to the Natural History Museum. Wisely someone has put a café at about the halfway point so that either on your way down, or your way back up, or preferably both, it's a good place to stop, rehydrate, and enjoy the view. Besides hydration it's where I got picture and video of the singing frogs. If you arrive in Funchal in the spring the sound you may think is a bird or a squirrel is actually a small frog seeking reproductive harmony.

At the Botanical Garden or any of the other gardens in and near Funchal, or really anywhere there is a rock wall, look for Madeira lizards. We sat in the Municipal Garden one afternoon enjoying the weather and the views when husband said, "You might want a picture of that." He pointed to the wall behind us which if you looked for a moment seemed to be moving. In nearly every crook and crevice was an aptly named Madeiran wall lizard. With a tail longer than it's three or four inch body it takes care of ants and other small insects. They are shy and harmless and truly native.

Another fear of heights challenge is the glass Skywalk at the Cabo Girão viewpoint, the highest cliff skywalk in Europe, similar in construction to the one at the Grand Canyon in Arizona. The views are tremendous and for those with a fear of heights you get points for a cardio workout without going more than a few steps. Extra credit if you manage to snap a picture of the farms 1,900 feet below you.

Husband and I have been learning Portuguese for four years now. We do okay at making ourselves understood. It's understanding what's being said to us in response that gives us grief. And on the island of Madeira we have encountered an accent that has us bamboozled. One native speaker told us, "It's because we don't open our mouths so much, and we talk through the nose. Even mainlanders have trouble with us." Well, it's something different. Native speakers are so kind when we speak to them. They slow down and break into English here and there. And mostly they want to know why we have been learning Portuguese. It's like learning Dutch. "You only learn Dutch if you're going to the Netherlands," is what a Dutch friend told us. We tell them we have a Portuguese daughter-in-law. She and our son thought we should retire to Portugal where it's cheap, warm, and is part of the EU making European travel so much easier and cheaper.

Portuguese is based on the fourth century Latin dialect left behind by the Romans when the issues of Empire sent them back to what would become Italy. The Iberian Peninsula, especially the portion that would become Portugal, was left isolated. This isolation gives us Portuguese, Catalan, Galician, and Castilian. None of these languages come up on anyone's list of "Easiest Languages to Learn."

Husband and I felt vindicated in our slow progress by the opening to 2016's *"Arrival"* where Amy Adams as the linguist about to be recruited by the government for interaction with newly arrived aliens tells her class that Portuguese is one of the most difficult languages to learn.

We struggle on, grateful for our Roku stick allowing us to stream English into our little stone house with a view of the sea.

Here's another bit about travel and technology. When we rented our home our tenants asked us to keep the cable in our name as they would be moving out so soon and back to their own house and cable package. We agreed because, why not? Xfinity kept telling us in their ads that we could take our entertainment with us anywhere. The caveat is that you can take it anywhere in the USA. Once you're out of the country you are subject to whatever agreements exist between countries for content. I thought we'd be able to log into our Xfinity account for our Santa Rosa address and watch what was being recorded back home. Not so. We can't even listen to the San Francisco CBS radio affiliate via radio.net. Our Roku stick has allowed us to watch Netflix, (an addiction to *"Designated Survivor"* has been the result) but not Masterpiece, or Masterpiece Mystery, or Discovery shows. I'll have a wonderful time with the reruns when we are back in the States. The British must make better deals because I can listen to and watch the BBC wherever we have traveled.

Back to the stone house by the sea. It was built in 1850 of thick volcanic rock. The view is a delight. Except for the shutters and the lack of screens. The bed in the master is quite squeaky, so I've left husband to it and I sleep in the twin in the child's room. Both rooms have French doors that open onto the ocean view balcony. The doors are covered by metal shutters. You can open the doors and the shutters, of course, but there is no screen door to keep out the flies. So, it's either doors closed with a view and no air, or doors and shutters open with an ocean breeze and a view swatting at flies. I choose flies every chance I get until husband says accusingly, one arm swinging at the air, "Your door is open, isn't it?" So I close the shutters and hide the view.

We tried without success to find a fly swatter. Fly spray was available everywhere, but we had to wait until we found a telescoping mini swatter in an Irish stationery store to battle the flies more effectively than with a rolled-up paper.

The black volcanic rock of which our house is made makes for a dramatic look in the areas where it has been left uncovered. It also keeps things cool. In a warmer time of year that would be a bonus. There is no heating here either. Madeira doesn't have a cold winter. The fireplaces we have seen are outside and used for cooking, maybe because they don't want to heat up the interiors. Living in a rock house means there is moisture in the air. When I open a cupboard that hasn't been opened for a few days, like the one that holds the pots and pans, there is a whiff of cave. It's not unpleasant, just a reminder that we are living in a "green" house made of black rock.

It is here on Madeira that both of us decide we need haircuts. It seems such an ordinary thing at home to call your stylist for an appointment and go in able to explain what you want. We didn't even try our Portuguese on the phone. We drove downtown and walked to the two salons we had found online and made appointments. When we returned at our appointed time one woman who spoke English did translation duty at the barber shop next door for husband, and then translated for me. It was unnerving to sit there hoping the translator's English was much better than my Portuguese and wondering how it would all turn out. Trust is a difficult thing, but all went well for both of us, probably because hairstylists work outside of language, going by feel and look.

When we have traveled in the past it was for two or three weeks. Even in that short time it was possible to get homesick. Long days in bad weather, or the vagaries of travel make one yearn for home, for ease and certainty. But those times are rare and pass quickly. The fascination of what is new and beautiful or new and delicious, or at least worth a try, pushes away the homesick spirit. Now, we're traveling for a year. There are things I miss with a depth of feeling I did not anticipate. I miss Trader Joe's. I miss In-N-Out. I miss Amy's. I miss My Deli on the way to my office where I could count on Ned making me the best-ever turkey and swiss on a soft roll. I miss Ross and Marshall's and Target. I also miss friends and family. Keeping in touch via email and WhatsApp is a big help, but it's not the same as hugs and kisses, and sitting in the same room with them. And I miss my routine. I miss going to the gym in the morning, my walk afterwards. I miss going to my office and sitting with clients. I miss the work. I miss the value of it. Here, though we are doing volunteer work, I still feel the edge of my personal tool of self-flagellation: "What are you doing that matters?" Our volunteer work matters, but there's not enough of it to make me feel I deserve to be at rest. And that is a personal fault, not the fault of travel. Husband gives me the lecture (ever briefer because we've been married for decades and arguments and discussions both get reduced to a shorthand) that tells me what matters is who I am, not how much I do. It brings tears to my eyes. Then, after a brief respite of agreeing with him, I go right back to trying to figure out how I can do more that will make a difference.

To get some practice driving a difficult car with a stiff manual transmission on interesting roads we drive out to Caniço, a town east of our neighborhood of São Gonçalo, and with easier beach access, but only if you like cable cars that plunge straight down the side of mountains. Our three-euro ride on the cable car of Complexo Balnear do Garajau was our third cable car thus far. It gives amazing views over the Atlantic and down to the beach where the restaurant roof says "Welcome to Paradise" as you slide on down. We had already feasted at the Frango da Guiia on seafood and chicken followed by the host insisting that we try Licor de Tangerina, a delicious Madeiran specialty. We neglected to take a bottle with us when we left for Ireland. Alas.

 Another day we took a drive around the western half of Madeira. It's a small enough island for that to be doable. We headed for Ribeira Brava on the Via Rapida (freeway) where we bought a knife for the kitchen at Estrelas Loucas, then had another delicious meal of seafood and chicken (at the poorly named Snack Bar and Pastelaria) sitting by the sea. We walked through a tunnel made from rocks formed in the volcanic action of the past to get to the port. It was like an art display in rock. From Ribeira Brava we went north on the inland road to São Vicente.

Caves kept popping up in our travels. In Oregon my cousins Jack and Vicki took us to the Rogue River Natural Bridge, a point where the Rogue disappears into an underground lava tube and then reappears downriver. It is a satisfyingly wild place, especially in the snow. Then there were the caves of Portimão, big enough to swallow a tour boat. Now on the north side of Madeira in São Vicente there are tamer, curated caves and it's nicely done. A tour guide takes groups through the caves and explains how they were formed, ages, type of rock, and all kinds of interesting miscellania. The cave now runs with water, and the pools are artfully lit, making for great pictures. When we were there boxes of wine were stored in the pools as an experiment to see if underwater storage would affect flavor of the local São Vicente wine, or perhaps just an excuse for a late summer feast.

From São Vicente we headed west and off to Porto Moniz where the natural swimming pools enticed, but the unseasonably cool air kept the pools empty. Ancient lava formed pools at the edge of the ocean, trapping sea water at high tide, making for safer and warmer water – just not this day. Down the western side of the island we saw many levadas from the road. Levadas are water channels built over the years to bring the abundant water from the mountain tops to the villages. Trails follow the path of the levadas as they need to be maintained. Walkers take advantage of these trails for beautiful hikes, some of them quite strenuous as they traverse narrow trails on steep mountainsides. We walked a mellower one recommended by Marco the owner of one of our favorite restaurants, Boa Vista.

We drove the eastern half another day finding ourselves on the highest point on the island where we looked for Africa but couldn't see it. We made audio recordings of the soughing of the wind through the trees and marveled at the diversity of landscapes on this small island. This particular spot is preserved as the Madeira Natural Park.

On our way back to civilization we found Casa de Chá do Faial. A wedding reception with a beautiful buffet was going on in the main part of the restaurant. We shared a garden-view room with several other couples and families listening in on the festivities. The food was, I'm repeating myself, delicious and the wine exceptional.

We finished the day by parking at the easternmost point of the island at the end of the road and continuing on foot. Here we saw the same kinds of solidified bubbles we had seen in the Algarve at Portimão by the lighthouse. These led us along a path of sorts to a spot where we decided to end our hike. The island peters out in the Atlantic like a finger pointing to Africa.

Another evening new friends João and Tracy along with Linda , another new British friend, take us to dinner at Restaurante Santo António in Câmara de Lobos. It is a higher class espetada restaurant, and like many others the menu is not on a piece of paper or ensconced in a binder. The waiter simply asks, "Chicken or meat?" It is assumed that you will want salad, chips, and fried corn. There is a menu for the wine, but João knows the place and asks for the homemade wine which arrives in an earthenware pitcher. It is a young red, thin, but tasty.

This is such a serious espetada restaurant that the hangers aren't brought to the table when you order. They are part of the table. If you come here, you are eating espetada.

A word about the fried corn. Santo António offered the best of anywhere we had it. It is, to the best of my translation ability, fried corn meal. It comes as a square of tasty fried goodness. The first time we had it we were sure it wasn't corn. Perhaps it was a bad translation on the menu. It could have been whipped potato that was subsequently fried. But a bit of research showed it was corn meal to which something has been added, something done to it, then it's fried and plated for your eating enjoyment. Not too much, please. It is not going to make anyone's Heart Healthy menu.

The meat and chicken, as everywhere else we ate, was delicious. Moist, tasty, and delightful. The salad had a few added items. At many restaurants on Madeira and on the mainland, a salad is lettuce, tomato, onion. Sometimes there are shredded carrots. On Madeira there might be corn, or cucumber. At Santo António's there were all of these items. Dressing is always the olive oil, vinegar, and salt do-it-yourself dressing.

The parking lot of Santo António is classic Madeiran: steep, narrow, curving, and no problem for locals. We were glad João was driving or we would have just driven on and missed the experience.

This was, we thought, the whole evening – dinner with new friends. But after we five were loaded into the car we were off to a true Poncha experience. Down the driveway to meet an oncoming BMW too long for any space here, but no. He brakes, reverses sideways into a tiny spot, and we were past him. Then off zooming up hills, down hills, around corners, and then up and up and up and around to a tiny place that is part snack bar, part rustic bar, part museum, A Venda do Andre. Poncha is a mix of aguardente de cana, honey, sugar, orange and/or lemon juice, and whatever fruit juice is offered. Traditionally it is lemon juice. You can buy a pre-mixed bottle, but don't. Find A Venda do Andre, or somewhere else where they pound the lemon in the bottom of the glass with a wooden stick, then add the sugar and honey for more mixing. Then the flourish of alcohol and fruit juice. It's slick, tasty, and has a serious punch.

Now it was growing dark. Linda was ready for home, and so was husband. But we were being toured by a native Madeiran eager to share in a brief time the best of his island.

Viana, back in Funchal, is an up-scale bakery/eatery. It sits on a corner with tables inside and out. Beautiful pastries, a wide selection of drinks from water and tea to coffees and liqueurs. Dinner is also on offer. At 9:30 on a Saturday night families were arriving to order dinner and dessert. We opted for coffees, a selection of mini-desserts, and brandy. Yes, brandy is served at the bakery. Hospitality is wide-ranging here.

Now we chummily load into the car once again. But still Linda doesn't get to go home. It's a quick tour of the downtown restaurant row, hotels (we meet the doorman, a friend of João's, at a hotel quite near the Savoy, or it might have been the Savoy: 'Come back for a drink!'), sightlines to the ocean, and the beauty of the tropical night.

Finally Linda is dropped at her apartment with a wonderful ocean view, and we're taken back to our car. Then it's off to find the Road of Death, which is easier to drive at night because headlights tell you before you round the corner if someone is coming.

A restaurant we found far too late in our stay is Restaurante Boa Vista. Marco, recently returned from decades in England, has opened a very nice place. At our first stop we were told they had just closed for the day. It was the first time we had been able to find a parking place near enough to make it worthwhile to stop. It is on Rua Conde Carvalhal, in an unusually wide stretch of the road, which means there is room for two bus stops, limiting parking. We finally found what we were looking for, a spot to park to get in for a late lunch. We were shown the last of the six items from which we could select three items for six euros. Husband, always the adventurous eater, ordered the pig parts stew, rice, and salad. I ordered the chicken, salad, potato combo. We both happily gobbled our meals. Marco came by to see how we were doing and asked if I had like the roasted potatoes. 'Oh, yes.' 'Then I'll bring you more.' And he did. I ate them happily and was nice enough to share with husband while we listened to Marco's story of immigration and return. Each time we went there the food was just as good, and Marco as friendly.

I can think of only one time I had anything close to 'not good,' and that was my fault because the two locals we were dining with advised me to take what the owner offered as the special of the day. But the translation led me to think it was going to be a turkey drumstick. I should have known it wouldn't be since the Portuguese butcher doesn't cut turkey like we do in America. They had delicious, juicy meat and I had an okay piece of pork.

"Computers are useless. They can only give you answers."

Pablo Picasso

Lesson re-learned. Always save and backup files before exiting. Microsoft upgrades glitch for me. I've already had one round of repairs done remotely from my nephew's office in California to my computer in Albufeira, Portugal. It took him longer than he expected but worked perfectly. Before we left the US Geremia the Great created two desktops on a new laptop purchased for this trip, one for husband and one for me. When Microsoft upgraded it worked fine for husband's side and denied me access to Word and pictures and deleted a couple of files that I hadn't emailed to myself. Geremia the Great did a work-around when he couldn't get the fix he wanted. So there were three desktops, husband's, the former "Kim", and a new "Kim McGrath". About a week ago Microsoft informed me there was a required update, and off we went again. It took hours to "upgrade." Then it repeated the denial of access for my side of things. Husband's side works fine, thank you. This is being written on husband's Word. I will send it to my email accounts and hope it doesn't get lost. Hopefully, Geremia the Great will have time soon to fit me in between his paying IT clients and give me a fourth version of "Kim" to work from.

I don't need to point out, but I am, that I do not have these kinds of problems with my iPad. The only fix needed in the three years I've had it was to turn it off, then on, to get it to unfreeze from a picture. That's it. Upgrades galore, and never a problem. Microsoft, please take a hint from Apple. Do something about your upgrades. I can't tell you how much money I've spent over the years before Geremia the Great entered our family, and since (because I do and will pay him), just to fix what Microsoft "upgrades." Apple has cost me nothing because no fixes were ever needed.

Back to Travel, closely related to travail, and to Latin for torture. I looked at the prospect of getting off Madeira and to Cork in one fell swoop. Not possible. I settled on getting to Lisbon one day, and then to Cork the next. It allowed us a night of sleep in an actual bed, not on a plane.

Getting out of Madeira wasn't too bad. Except that we are traveling now with this wonderful card that gets us into airport lounges. Lounges are a delight, even the indifferent ones, like JFK's Terminal 5 in New York. Every bit of all passenger waiting areas in airports everywhere should be a lounge. Real seating, not molded plastic. Couches even, to stretch out on. Food, drink, well-appointed bathrooms, sometimes showers or beds, private rooms for phone conversations. There is always a board showing the flight information for those folks who are checked into the lounge. This requires you to keep checking for updates. In these two days of travel we both got too lounged and came to the first flight from Madeira when passengers had already begun boarding. Oops. Lesson learned. We'll pay attention next time.

But, no problem. We hurried across the tarmac and made our flight. From Lisbon airport to our hotel via taxi was no problem. The Holiday Inn I had booked because it was closest to the airport is not like any Holiday Inn I've checked into in the US. Breakfast, not a continental affair, is included in the room rate. There is an actual restaurant in the hotel where we had a good dinner and chose from a decent wine selection served by wait staff in traditional black and white attire with a white towel for the bottle. I kept checking the reflection in the window that, indeed, said "Holiday Inn."

Next morning another taxi to the airport for a British Airways flight to London where we would connect with an Aer Lingus flight to Cork.

Lisbon airport was full and busy. At check-in the clerk told us we should go straight to Passport Control as there were long lines everywhere. When she arrived for work the security line had been backed up to the airport entrance. It was much shorter now and we made the mistake, only the first of the day, of thinking that once we passed security we were okay. Not smart. We were leaving Portugal for a layover in England with a final destination of Ireland. We should have gone to Passport Control next. We didn't. We lounged at a very nice lounge.

Lisbon airport isn't huge, but we didn't want to run through the airport. We did though. We ran through the airport after a long and fractious wait in a very slow line at Passport Control. People afraid of missing their flights began cutting the line. The mix of cultures had different responses to this. Some ignored the bad behavior of their fellow humans. Some pointed it out in loud voices to their companions. Representatives from various airlines were coming in the room with their lists, calling out passenger names, and then saying only that since they knew their passengers were in line for Passport Control they would do their best to coordinate with Air Traffic to hold the plane for them. This unnerved even more people and the line cutting amped up. This time a local woman had had enough. She called a Security person over and told him the story in Portuguese. He made his way through the line and spoke with one group of offenders to no avail. When husband and I finally found ourselves at the front of the line his shoe was pulled off by the foot of a woman who had been about three turns of the snaking line behind us when we first saw her. Voices were raised behind us at the unfairness, but she shot into a line and her passport was inspected. Our time at the Passport Control window was less than ten seconds. The agent took the passport from my hand, and immediately handed it back. Husband got the same treatment along with a thumb pointing at the door and "Go!" We went. The group of line cutters passed us by running for their own flight. It wasn't our flight, so we don't know if their plane waited for them. Ours did. The same clerk who had checked us in was now at the gate. "Didn't I tell you? It's crazy today" she said. "I'm supposed to be closing the gate. Hurry, hurry!" The lift right behind the gate doesn't work. To board our plane we must descend more stairs to find we are snaking around again, this time to board a bus. A bus where one of the line jumpers sits chatting with his friend. Husband says, "That was getting ugly back there." "Yes," line jumper says. "They needed a lesson. That's why I made my move." He's an elderly very British gentleman. We were surprised when he did the line jumping, and more surprised to hear his defense. Though in one sense he was quite right. There was a roomful of increasingly frantic passengers and only four agents who at various times had conversations with each other to the exclusion of whoever was at their window. There may have been some major security event happening of which we were not aware. Not sure what could have been done other than having more employees at the windows.

I had reserved flights with a long layover in LHR because prior experience there made me certain we didn't want a connection that was too tight. As it was our five-hour layover was almost completely taken up with errors and security. On previous trips that involved transferring at Heathrow we had experienced the full range of waiting onboard the plane for a bus that was running late, that then took us on a long ride (we thought maybe we had actually landed at another airport and were being transported to Heathrow via bus), dropped us at a train, that led us to elevators and escalators and a tremendously long walk that got us to the gate when boarding was nearly over. That was a connection of just under two hours. It's why I chose flights that gave us more than five hours.

First error at Heathrow: an airport employee at the end of the Passport line, spotted our passports as we passed by and directed us to the Non-EU Passport line. We took him at his word and shouldn't have. An hour later, after a great conversation with an American married to a Brit who was flying in from his latest gig as a stand-up comedian, the Immigration official told us we were in the wrong line and should be upstairs in Connections and Security. As we exited there were now three BA employees directing folks to Connections who commiserated with us, apologized, and gave correct directions.

Something about our hand baggage triggered a security search of our bags. They were short of employees to do the search and had to call someone in. This took a while. The woman wasn't new to what she was doing, but she did have to ask for advice from a passing employee in regard to a medical device we carry with us. One of our carry-ons has all of our electronics in it, plus husband's meds, laptop, husband's phone, husband's tablet, cables, connectors, external hard drive, etc. The other bag is a Cpap machine, which is exempt from carry-on rules, but not from inspection. The third bag is my giant bag in which I keep my tablet and purse and the miscellania of airports and train stations.

Every time we go through security it is a different list of requirements. Sometimes we have to remove shoes, and other times not. At times we have been told to pull out all electronics, or only the laptop, or the laptop and the tablet, or leave everything in the bag, please.

Flustered from being in the wrong line for so long, worried that time was dwindling away, as we had been bussed to the airport again, husband didn't remove the laptop from the electronics bag before putting it in the bin. We think this is what set everything off and made us suspect.

Even with all this we once again took time to check in at the lounge, have a drink and a small meal, freshen up. And once again we cut it too close. Husband is suffering from a side effect of a powerful antibiotic given him more than a year ago for pneumonia. His Achilles tendon is brittle and has lost its flexibility. This makes walking difficult. And here we were realizing we were cutting it too fine and trying to dash like the young people we are only in our own heads. Our carry-on bags had to be checked at the gate as the flight was full and there was no room in the overhead bins. Husband took out the problematic laptop and onboard we went. Despite miscalculations, lounging too long, and bad ankles we made the flight and landed in Cork on time.

Ireland

There is a song claiming Ireland has 40 shades of green, which has been disproved by science, according to our Irish friend. There are 40,000 shades of green in Ireland – so he claims. I'm not counting. All I know is that green, lovely, beautiful, energizing, enlivening green is everywhere, even though we arrived in an unexpected heat wave. We left Madeira on a 72F day with the locals bundled up in long pants and coats. In Cork it was 72F, and the locals were in shorts. Mike, the man who came to pick us up, was wearing shorts and sandals. It's all about location and perspective.

Mike drove us to the house we are renting from a friend of a new friend we made who was vacationing in Albufeira. The owners are off to London for a building project and were in need of someone to watch their house. We were in need of a house. Done! We are in a lovely home ten minutes outside Fermoy, County Cork. The backyard of a couple of acres, some of which we will be mowing, looks down on a valley of green – I've mentioned the green green green – grass and trees that rises up to more green hills in the distance. It is peaceful and gorgeous. Our neighbors are young bulls, sadly probably soon to be meat, but for now they are young enough to be friendly and curious.

Mike asks if we'd like a drink before settling in, and we say 'sure.' This is new for us, especially new for husband. Travel is unwinding our clocks and inhibitions. At home if someone had said to us after a long day's travel "Come out for a drink?" we would have said "No". The lure of pajamas and a washed face along with a bit of "What's on?" or a chapter in my book would have been more alluring. But we were on our first night in town and a local was asking us out.

He waited while the aunt of the couple we are renting from gave us the keys and showed us the house, and the loads of goodies she and the couple had left for us. Chocolate, sparkling water, bread, butter, eggs, cookies (AKA biscuits here), tea, coffee, and other things we've eaten and now can't recall.

Off we went to Noola's, on a corner of Patrick Street. Tiny. Old. Linoleum floor. It's not been re-decorated since whoever laid down the lino did that job. Noola herself is quiet and smiling. In an instant we were absolutely somewhere else completely, and in a particularly wonderful way. Husband is convinced to try a Guinness though he claims to not like the dark. He is converted. I opt for a half pint of beer. It's been a long hot day and the beer rejuvenates what we've sweated out. In the small communal room off the tiny bar we join Patrick, the town's retired barber, and Mike's son Thomas. Mike knows Patrick because he used to get his hair cut in Patrick's shop.

We had been told about Irish craik, the Irish conversations that happen spontaneously almost anywhere, but especially where there is beer and time. Patrick, Mike and Thomas between them give us some details about the area, about the place, about themselves, and about people we won't ever meet. Paddy, the large man. No, he was a large man, and his Honda 50, a fine machine. If you could get one now, what a fine machine you would have. But Paddy he was such a big man and his 50 was so small that when he went up the hill back home all you saw was Paddy floating, floating up the hill.

I've done the story no justice. It has to be told with an Irish lilt and subtle gestures. It reduced us to tearful laughter and the wish that we could have known Paddy and that we had lived here our whole lives and that we could stay in Noola's listening to Patrick and Mike. But a glance at my personal reminder of the 21st century showed that it was 11:00! Way past husband's bed time. The sun had just gone down, the sky still the soft blue-black of post-sunset, and we had thought it was 9:00-ish. We had not accounted for the fact that southern Ireland is at a higher latitude than the US-Canada border and summer's longest day of the year was not far off.

So Mike took us home and we slid into sleep.

The rest of our time here has gone as well as the first night in Noola's. Mike has become a friend, tour guide, advisor, and mentor in all things Irish. His people have been here since before the year 902 and by then one of them was king.

One benefit of arriving during an Irish drought, other than how happy the locals are with the sunshine, is it makes being a tourist easier – no rain. Mike takes us to see Kinsale, a wildly historical place, already being an important port in 1381. Then we are off on a short boat ride to Garinish Island in Bantry Bay to see an enchanted island garden. The enchantment pales only slightly when we walk up into the 19th century Martello Tower, used in World War II as an observation point and wonder at the contrast of the great beauty here and the horror of war. Though we didn't see them, Garinish is home to a pair of Sea Eagles. The once abundant natives were extinct in the wild by the 20th century, so this re-introduced pair creates much hope for their recovery.

Another day Mike drives us through the Vee where the rhododendrons that have naturalized over much of southern Ireland are beautifully in bloom, up the hills, down the valleys, surrounding the creeks, pesky but gorgeous. We drive a portion of the Ring of Kerry, but against the tour bus traffic, thus ensuring that we arrive at a view spot after the groups have left, which is a good way to find yourself nearly alone staring off at the ancient green and rocky vistas that so soothe the soul.

While driving along the Blackwater River one day I find an estate home with my family name on the gate. It's down the road from a large home where we got a tour from the aging owner. We saw the 'For Sale' sign and drove in to the generous courtyard for a look. Her home is a grand three-story with cellars, views of the river and valley, and the kind of graciously curving staircase you'd expect in such a place. Though it's in decay and would need at least one hundred thousand euros in work it is still in the million-euro range.

When we told friends about our accidental meeting and tour, we were told that we were on the English side of the river, where officers and garrisons were housed during the occupation. No doubt the reason my family name was there is that I'm more English than Irish. But with the kindness of the Irish I was assured that since my great-grandfather lived in the North before the border it wouldn't be a problem, and, well, the English did get around.

Toilets

A toilet is such a common plumbing fixture that you'd think there couldn't be anything to wonder about here. Move along, please. But, no. Like so many things, everyone does it differently. Things have become more uniform since my first visit to Europe when I was advised to "Push, pull, turn, yank whatever isn't porcelain. That might flush it." Even now when multinational corporations have homogenized so many things that it's hard to find something unique to bring back as a present, there is wide variety in plumbing. In case you're wondering, if I hand you some German chocolate as a gift when I get home, check it for the Cost Plus sticker. It's cheaper there than in Germany.

But back to the bathroom. My goal in using a toilet is to get things in the water, get it flushed, and get out. Toilets in certain parts of northern Germany offer the opportunity to get up close and personal with one's excreta. It's a matter of health, I'm told. It's a matter of, "How do you flush that?" for me. It is also a cleaning issue, and if you don't get it right, you're in trouble. Some toilets in Portugal were little more than a porcelain bowl over a straight porcelain pipe, like a dentist's spit bowl. If someone wanted to check their leavings there wouldn't be a way except by scooping it up. There is still variety in handles; some you push, some you pull, but I haven't come across one on this trip that I can't figure out. Being a native Californian accustomed to drought I haven't used any that would meet the low-flow flush requirements of home. Some gush like a broken fire hydrant with a frightening burst of water. And staying in old parts of town means you're staying with old plumbing as well. Old pipes, smelly pipes. On Madeira husband, sniffs the hint of loose plumbing pipes and having worked for a water treatment plant construction company wonders where they treat the stuff. A lawyer turned businessman we were talking with at lunch laughed and pointed to the sea. "About a mile out there," he said. "I was afraid of that," husband mumbled in reply. Another reason, besides the unseasonable cold, to stay out of the water.

Some of the plumbing is so antique that it can't handle paper. As in Mexico, there's a bin beside the toilet for your used paper. Whoever makes the small metal cylinder can with the foot pedal has made a fortune. They're everywhere in Portugal and Ireland. In Dublin where we went for a convention at a high-end hotel there was one in the bathroom. Not for the toilet here, thank you. Irish toilets handle the paper. They handle just about anything given the high volume of water with each flush. "Ah, there's plenty more where that came from," said the owner of the B&B regarding the water at our last visit. At that time California was in a major drought and at home we were using buckets to catch the cold water that came while we waited for hot water to shower with. Then we used the bucket to flush the toilet. Of course, only after we had used it at least twice. "If it's yellow, let it mellow."

While California takes quite a while to get to drastic conservation measures, Ireland hits the drastic mark after only a couple of weeks. A nearby village has run out of water, and is having it trucked in to the village water tower. No watering with a garden hose. No washing the car with a hose. If you have one. The home we're in doesn't have one, hasn't needed one. As things got drier we decided to water, but not finding a hose we ended up with buckets filled at the spigot. We came to Ireland for a cool, green summer. It looks more and more like California spring every day. Somebody is probably already importing low-flow fixes. Soon there will be no more gushing Irish toilets.

Meanwhile the locals are snapping pictures of brown lawns. A rare sight!

Electrical

In the two Irish houses we stayed in there was no shortage of outlets. We did have to remember to move the tiny switch to turn the plug on. My experience in Europe has been that bathroom light switches are on the wall outside the door. My brother explained this to me, the 220 volts there versus the 110 in the USA making it more sensible to have it outside the room. I cannot keep the science of it straight. What I do know is that growing up my brother would have gleefully put us all in the dark at inopportune moments given that chance.

Crows

England has a long history with ravens. Visit the Tower of London and you'll hear the story of ravens and the continuation of the monarchy. But I hadn't expected there would be such a variety of crows and ravens around. At our home in Santa Rosa we are blessed with a small local flock of vocal crows. Husbands likes to call them on a summer evening and watch them swirl in the sky above us like a vortex of black.

No members of the Corvid family (crows, ravens, jays, etal) have lovely voices, but they are amazingly smart. Here in Ireland there is a variety of colors, sizes, and habits. Our country lane is home to numerous crows and their calls are impossible to miss. Husband is sorry he didn't pack his crow call to see how many might respond to an American accent. When I take a walk down the lane I always call up a "Hello!" to them which usually makes them quiet down for a moment. One day I did this as I left the house and passed under their particular group of trees. On my way back they were settled in the trees and I called up another "Hello!" There was some hopping about and then, plop, plop, a gift of crow poop on each shoulder. I laughed up at them not knowing if this was coincidence, insult, initiation, or warning.

Friends invite us to a Brazilian barbecue. We speak European Portuguese, but we can get along if the Brazilians speak slowly enough. There are Brazilians in Ireland because they like meat perhaps more than the Irish do. A large meat packing company with locations around Ireland has some sort of arrangement for bringing in Brazilian butchers to work in their plants, so there are plenty of Portuguese speakers. It could be argued that there are two languages: Brazilian and Portuguese. There are many similarities and many differences, some more culturally based. European Portuguese use more formal speech than Brazilians. What is everyday Brazilian usage can seem disrespectful to mainlanders, though not to us as we are just struggling to keep up.

The first rule we broke was arriving on time. We knocked on the door just past the appointed time to the surprise of the hosts. We helped with the setup and waited for others to arrive, some as much as two hours later. At some point there is a formal start to the meal, but no one sits at the table. The meat is on the grill and that is where the men are, turning, poking, testing and tasting. The neighbor cat finds a seat on the wall above the grill and is fed tidbits by the softhearted amongst us. It was obvious these Brazilian men didn't think good meat should be wasted on cats. Salads and vegetables are available, but plates are filled with delicious meat and sausage. Salads are only a sideline, even the one made with treasured ingredients from the Brazilian market.

Brazilians aren't the only ones with their own market in town. One afternoon on my way home I remembered something we needed for dinner, and spotting a parking space – a coup in itself – near a little market that I hadn't tried, I parked and went in to find the shopkeeper and I were in trouble. Polish only. I tried wandering the aisles, but the jars and cans were in Polish. A large pastry display had been well picked over. The shopkeeper pointed at it and smiled, nodding her head and waving her hand over it. I took it to mean that they were good and I should take one. I bought some hard Polish candies and one of the pastries and went home without what I needed but feeling well-traveled. The woman was right, the pastry was delicious.

That Ireland had welcomed these two nationalities, along with the diversity we saw in Dublin and Cork, made us hopeful that we might be able to get a visa extension.

Death

I am wrestling with my separation anxiety. Death is the biggest separation anxiety there is. Back home the best ER in the county is two miles from my door. The other hospital, Kaiser Medical, is about four miles away. My office was less than a half mile from Memorial Hospital. Life Flight helicopters would fly over headed for the helipad, loud enough to stop clients mid-sentence. Then we'd say something like, "Well, things could be worse, I guess." Then for me a silent prayer and adding "I didn't have to be taken to Memorial in a helicopter today" to my list of daily gratitudes.

But I start to worry about that little bump on the inside of my right elbow. Or I worry about the side effects of husband's medication. And then I'm wondering how far it is to the hospital in Cork (the nearest to us in Fermoy) under emergency conditions. Then I start the self-talk I would recommend to clients. How are you feeling? Why are you feeling it? What just happened? What's your plan? Like some clients I can't find what happened that triggered the feeling of impending doom. Oh, wait, yes, I can. We've got a move-out date. Our landlords have an unexpected opportunity to come back and repair a roof leak and the interior damage it caused to one bedroom, all of which happened before we came along. We are back to trying to figure out where to go next. Not being planners creates anxiety, which for me leads to thoughts of dismemberment or at least mashing of body parts in an unsuitable way, and ultimately death. I find myself wondering how husband or I would get the other's body back to the States, or if we can get cremated as visitors. I don't believe anything lives on after me, nor that the body is precious, but for reasons I don't understand, I don't want my ashes left behind. Except for a handful I've made my husband promise to scatter somewhere in Hyde Park in London. He's known that for years, so this fear of tragic death is nothing new, not inherently attached to travel itself, nor to getting older.

To counteract my anxiety we go for a walk in the Glenabo Forest looking for a waterfall that the drought has dried up. Still lots of lovely trees and ferns, a trilling creek, cool air, evidence of boars living here, and time to think in our forest bath.

Immigration

Our attempt to get a Stamp 0 visa for a one-year extension of our stay in Ireland has pointed up the flaws inherent in a world with borders. There's always somebody managing them, making rules about who gets in, who has to go, how long you stay, how long before you return. US citizens get 90 days out of 180 in the EU. We get 6 months out of twelve in the UK.

Imagine a world without borders. If you like Ireland or France or Portugal and you can find a home someone wants to rent to you or sell to you, you're welcome. Stay as long as you like. Right now I have a stack of papers showing I have friends in Ireland, a home to live in, money in the bank, liquid assets in case of need, have applied for Irish health insurance, have a valid US passport, have never been arrested in my home city, and have reasonable health. This required a visit to an Irish accountant, a visit to an Irish insurance agency, letters from our doctors in Santa Rosa, and for my sister-in-law to go to the Santa Rosa Police Department with cash and a copy of a letter from us asking for a Visa Clearance Certificate. Something we did not explain to Morris, the nice Immigration Officer in the Fermoy Guarda Station, is that the Clearance Certificate from Santa Rosa only tells Ireland that husband and I have never been arrested in Santa Rosa. In Ireland that same kind of letter would mean that we had not been arrested anywhere in Ireland. They accept our letter, which if read carefully, tells the exact truth that we have never been arrested in Santa Rosa. If they asked for an FBI clearance we'd be years in the process, though equally clean in the end.

We must also write a letter stating our reason for requesting a visa extension in Ireland. Because it's so darn beautiful here that it brings tears to my eyes. Because I like the conviviality of Irish people. Because I like green. Because I like cows for neighbors. Because turning a corner and seeing that view of a green Irish valley pebbled with cows or sheep or horses makes me gasp with happiness. Because I want to see if I can find where my family actually came from. Because I haven't had enough of Ireland yet. Because it feels like home. Because I'm tired of suitcases and airport security and uncertainty.

And yet, home. I want home. "Dear Dr J, I want to come home."

Onward, ever onward, searching through the byways of Irish bureaucracy. You need an Irish bank account to pay the premium on the health insurance. No cash payments accepted for health insurance. You can't get the bank account until you have a policy coverage letter showing a policy number and current Irish residence, and a passport. You must have A and B to get C, but you can't get A until you have B and C.

Ah well, we're fluidity itself. While we'd like to stay in Ireland, would mourn having to leave, we have other places on our travel list. So we will continue to invest the cash to see if we are acceptable to the Irish government. If not, it was an exercise in reality. Right now reality is uncertainty for us. Our life is a lot like the A/B/C situation. If we get kicked out of Ireland, we'll go to Germany, or Scotland, or perhaps Northern Ireland. Maybe we'll go to New York. There are museums and sites I'd like to see, and it's actually closer from here than from California. So many choices that it's driving me crazier.

Meanwhile, the drought is doing its damage to the landscape. A bit of rain two days ago was a real relief. Immediately things began to green back up. But we're still a few more good storms away from recovery. Fires rage all over Europe. People burned to death in Greece. The Arctic Circle is hot, relatively speaking, and fires rage in Sweden.

The San Francisco Chronicle Travel section on a Sunday in July devotes itself to #vanlife, in which they seek to explain the reality of living small and traveling. Erik Ekman wrote about the ideal length of time for living in a van. "You start to spin out at about six months," he says. We've been on the road since December 30, 2017, coming up on seven months. We haven't lived in a van, but have rented homes, stayed with friends, and family. We're both at the point where if we had a home to go to, we would, even though we love Ireland and have enjoyed meeting new people, trying new foods, seeing new places.

On past trips what tells me I am done and ready for home is when I find myself near tears because I am not sure where my toothbrush is and I'm just too frustrated to want to work it out. Travel has shown me how much a creature of habit I am. Husband is, if anything, worse. He would prefer not to leave home based on the possibility that at some future time he will not know where his toothbrush is. This seems trivial. To non-travelers, and to me when I've been home too long and I forget how bad that travel moment feels, it seems unimportant. So much time and energy is put into a trip, and then to feel like all you want is to be at home where you know where everything is, and how everything works, and where to go to get the best vegetables, or what restaurant has the best Happy Hour deal without having to ask, to not need assistance every time you negotiate a bureaucratic tangle. Or not having bureaucratic tangles because you are home. You don't need a passport or a visa or permission or clearance or approval or a ticket, please. And if you do need something out of the ordinary, it's perhaps a few frustrating phone calls, and then, mystery solved, you get on with life. Travel complicates. Phone service, grocery carts, parking regulations, car rentals, food itself. To tip or not to tip. Buying clothes. Dry cleaners. Mail. And we are feeling this in a country where our struggle with language is rather minor.

Then I remind myself that we have already spent three months in Portugal where we did struggle with the language. We've done that battle. We can do it again. And if we get our visa extension in Ireland then we can revel in the eccentricities of English from a safe haven.

Today, after my dashing from bank to insurance agency back to the bank, then a quick stop at M. Spillane's Butcher for the most luscious roasted chicken, and a dash into Lidl for lettuce I'm home to catch the breeze, watch the clouds scoot past, and monitor the bullocks meandering in the pasture at the bottom of the gentle slope we sit atop. Husband pours me part of his Tiger beer – excellent- and we breathe in the peace, something to do with ions, positive or negative. I can't keep that straight. Sitting under an Irish sky is for me akin to sitting on North Beach in San Clemente, or Water's Edge at Lake Tahoe. It's like being washed, massaged, and moisturized.

A rain flurry has just passed. The air is clear and refreshing. There's a hiking trail just a few minutes away. I'm going to take a forest bath, rejuvenate the brain cells, and remind myself how very, very fortunate husband and I are to be on the road.

"Dear Dr J, I still want to come home, but not yet."

Our friend Mike took us to Kilkenny Castle for a tour and then on to meet friends of his. In the castle library I noted that one of the volumes was titled "Manners of America." When I pointed this out to husband there were comments from others in the room. The docent said he thought it was a small book. Our friend's daughter asked if it was a blank book. The German family chuckled. Even when we're behaving, we're getting the Ugly Americans treatment. How do you answer that? It's something to joke about because it's often true, because it's a cliché, or because Americans are clichés. Dave Barry once wrote about his family's travels in Japan (*Dave Barry Does Japan*) wherein he reported feeling like a water buffalo amidst the well-mannered, quiet, and shorter than he Japanese. It is a feeling I relate to often while traveling. Not because I'm tall, nor unmannerly, but because there is often a feeling of having missed something. We are not traveling with an etiquette specialist like politicians and executives do. We must use the amused or amazed expressions of the locals to tell us we've blundered down to the water hole in the wrong way. Sometimes they tell us kindly and sometimes we're a joke at which we get to laugh also. And sometimes I wonder what just happened. I know we have laughed at or joked with foreign visitors about their missteps. I vow to be more careful in the future to be sure my foreign visitors know I am laughing with them, noting the oddity of American ways, not laughing at them for being water buffalo amidst the gazelles, or perhaps gazelles amongst the water buffalos. Because frankly, none of us can claim superiority, only difference.

Groceries

Anywhere I've been in the US shopping carts are free to use. They may have some mechanism to stop them at the edge of the store property, but they are free to use. Something I had not noticed on prior European trips, probably because I was only picnic shopping, is the charge for shopping carts, or trolleys as they're called here. There is an ingenious lock mechanism that keeps the stock of trolleys chained together outside the store. A coin inserted in the slot releases the chain holding a trolley to its fellows and off you go into the store. Once you've emptied your purchases into your car, bike, etc, you return to the trolley corral, click the chain from a fellow cart into yours and, voila! your coin is yours again. So there's no charge for using a shopping trolley, just the problem of always needing a coin to be able to go shopping. This cuts out the employee whose job in the US is to collect the carts from wherever customers leave them outside and bring them in. It also solves the problem of trolleys banging into the side of your car, or those trolleys that might simply be abandoned once they're finished with, blocking up parking spaces or traffic aisles. Something about wanting a coin back keeps people putting trolleys back where the store wants them. I like that aspect of the shopping trolley on a chain.

Which brings me back into the store with the coin still in the slot. In the US it's quite the norm to stand around looking bored while the checker whips your goods across the scanner and either packs them into a bag or passes them onto a bagger who does that job for you. It's become increasingly common to bag things yourself, as many do at Trader Joe's, but it is not expected. In both Ireland and Portugal on this trip I was reminded of prior shopping trips where I quickly learned that the only help I was going to get from the checker was the scanning of my purchases. If I needed to buy a bag, he or she might hand it to me, or more likely, point out where I could get it. On those trips I was never buying more than a picnic meal. On this trip we're trying to live here, which means real grocery trips. Which means, it turns out, there is a hectic checkout process. Clerks are often on chairs and only one store we used, Riordan SuperValu, had occasional baggers. Your purchases are moved to a small area where you're expected to scoop them back in your cart or into your bags. In many stores there is a shelf near the checkout where you can bag your items after purchase. When the checker is finished scanning, they wait for you to finish. One checker slid a man's mayo bottle right onto the floor where its lid broke. He sent his son off for a replacement while the checker kept scanning. At least no charge was made for the replacement. Minutes later my chocolate bar met a similar fate. I didn't care if it had cracked inside. I did mind that it had been on the floor, but, oh well. Such is life at the European checkout. If you're slow about getting your things bagged or back in the cart, no worries. The checker simply waits, as do the folks behind you.

In Ireland conversation is important. So I've been in line behind folks having a good conversation, customer and checker catching up with each other, "Now, how is your Aunt?", or making plans for the evening. No matter that the order has been scanned, bagged, and possibly paid for. No apologies made to those in line behind. And as far as I can tell, no complaints from those in line behind this friendliness. Speed is not of the essence, people are. Good lesson for an Ugly American to remember.

There are an abundance of riverside rest stops all along the Blackwater and its tributaries. At these tables you can picnic or have your morning cuppa while enjoying the views. Besides this natural generosity of Ireland we have enjoyed a number of curated buildings and gardens. Muckross House is a must. We enjoyed the gardens, hundreds of years old with enormous trees and shrubs with acres of freedom in which to be full grown, and tremendous views. No regrets that we never got in the house.

Ardmore, in County Waterford, is home to Ireland's only hotel with a Michelin starred restaurant. That's not why we were there. Mike and part of his family took us to do the walk that leads from the beach up to the 12th century round tower and the ruins of a cathedral that contains Ogham stones, upright stones with lines carved into them that generally translate to personal names. They date to as early as the 4th century. Possibly they served as property boundary markers. No charge to visit the church yard, just the expenditure of energy to get up the hill and stand in an ancient place contemplating life.

On another drive Mike takes us to the Master McGrath monument. Master McGrath was a much-loved greyhound who won many races in the 1860s. While you would think a monument to a long dead dog would be an obscure monument, we were asked several times, after people heard our last name, if anyone had taken us to see the statue. Horses and dogs are very beloved here.

In our travels we saw caves on the Rogue River in Oregon, at Portimão in Portugal, at Saõ Gonçalo on Madeira, and in County Tipperary at the Mitchelstown Cave. Mitchelstown Cave is a complex system discovered in 1833 by a man who dropped his crowbar and in moving boulders to retrieve it caught sight of a chamber. At the farthest point in there is a vast chamber where tour groups are asked if anyone wants to sing. The acoustics are wonderful and musical events are regularly held there.

Another Tipperary historic site is the Ormond Castle, which we visited because, like so many sites in Ireland, there is a family connection for Mike. Unlike other places he has visited, no free entry was offered him on the day we stopped in. After our tour we strolled into the village and indulged in a beer in a cool pub. So civilized.

"What gives value to travel is fear... At that moment we are feverish but also porous, so that the slightest touch makes us quiver to the depths of our being."

Albert Camus, French author

Words were said. Travel is hard. Planning is hard. We're not well-matched in our approach to travel planning. I'd like to have it all tied up, with reservations made, boarding passes waiting in my Inbox. Long-term rentals are not so easy to come by in small towns such as the one we want to go to for a month and I grow more and more frustrated. Husband prefers to wing it, waiting for something to turn up, someone to offer something. Usually it happens as husband likes it. We know somebody who knows somebody who has a friend who has a place that can be ours. It's about to happen again. But only after my gut-twisted rant that "We have to make plans now!"

Our time in this particular green haven is coming to its close in a few days. The landlords we have never met are due to return. As yet we have no confirmed place to stay next. I remind myself that I have a powerful credit card with all kinds of features, the simplest of which is to reserve a room at the nearest airport hotel. Not ideal, but doable. What's the worst that could happen? I'm not a woman traveling solo in a hostile country with cash only. We're currently in Ireland, a civilized and hospitable nation. Distance is perhaps the worst impediment. But rental cars come with unlimited mileage and a Spar market is never far away.

Confirmation comes via a phone call that once again husband has pulled it off. We have the home of a friend of a friend who has gone back to France leaving their Irish home still unsold, and they will be glad of a month's rent. We will be moving to Nenagh, County Tipperary, in a week. And a friend of this friend has an auto repair shop from which he rents cars privately. Deal done. Crisis averted. Marriage saved. Credit card out of danger.

We will be heading off to what might be our last new house in Ireland as we will be returning to the cottage in Fermoy after roof repairs are completed. Returning there will be the first time in a year that we pull up to a house and know what's inside. Because it is a family home it is well stocked and comfortable. Other places we have rented have been a spectrum of 'Wonderful!' to Really?'

As you peruse the zillions of pictures of houses, apartments, cabins, treehouses, and rooms you might like to rent just remember that flexibility will serve you well. Whether you need that flexibility when it comes to the seating, the beds, the kitchen, the shower, just know that you will need it. A good traveler is as flexible as a plumber's snake. If you are staying long enough in one place and find you really need a certain something, be prepared to shop. Consider it a part of your education, your cultural immersion, in your new location. For our various temporary homes we bought numerous kitchen knives, scissors, graters, peelers, and a frying pan. We appreciated those landlords who supplied enough: seating, linens, towels, hangers, and kitchen tools. We thought it a bonus if we opened cupboards and found spices, flour, oil, tea, and other miscellania. If each house also had a good blow dryer, it would be perfect because they take up valuable suitcase space. One thing I always wish there were more of is hooks on the back of doors, but I'm not going to screw those in.

We have heard from the local Immigration officer that we have an additional sixty days to wait for an answer from Irish Immigration as to whether or not we can stay for up to one year from the date of approval as visitors. We're not sure we'll stay that long, but we'd like the option. We've made friends here. We like the weather and the green, green, greenness of it.

We thought we had grown tired of Madeira's omnipresent espetada, but we find ourselves salivating at the memory of the delicious chunks of chicken or beef hanging in front of us while a plate of salad awaited it's oil and vinegar bath, and warm bread still lingered in our mouths. Here in Fermoy we make sure not to miss Enzo's (Patrick Street, Fermoy) Tuesday pasta special. Don't be fooled by the chippy face of this small restaurant. Yes, you can get chips, burgers, and other fast foods. Enzo the owner and Felice, his son-in-law, are Italian, and they can cook. The pizzas are made to order and the best around. You can buy the dough if you ask. Felice cooks his specials based on what he learned from his mother and from culinary school. We always order two portions, share one, and eat the other for lunch or dinner the next day. Generous portions of homemade pasta dishes from a region we're not familiar with means we look forward to Tuesdays with delight.

Felice shared some of his father's pepper oil with us. Once a year he gets a new batch from his dad and we got the tail end of this year's batch. It surely adds the heat to whatever you're cooking. Husband likes to use it with his scrambled egg, and anything else he plates.

While out shopping one day I stopped at the deli in the back of the Centra market and ordered a chicken sandwich to take home to share with husband as lunch. 'Did I want salad with that?' 'Yes, please'. 'Potato?' Well, it is Ireland, so of course it's potato salad. It takes a moment for me to realize that the deli woman is slathering the potato salad on the bread. I start to protest, then stop because I don't want to be the fussy American lady. Perhaps, I think, she's new here. I'll scrape it off at home. Turns out that it is quite good, and quite common. We ordered it the same way a few more times. In many groceries you can find people in the deli who are graduates of culinary school doing the cooking, not just opening packages.

Another day our friend called and asked us to meet him and a group of friends at the Amber for lunch. The only Amber we knew was a fuel station. "That's the place," he said. Saying no more, we thought we would meet him there and then go wherever it was he had in mind for lunch. The Amber was where we ate. Inside, past the registers for paying for your fuel, was a sparkling deli serving all things deli as well as tea and then the Hillbilly's Restaurant. Like elsewhere in Europe it is possible to have a good meal where you get fuel for your car. Mike wanted us to have the Tuesday special: two snack packs of chicken and chips for the price of one. For about 5 euros we got four pieces of excellent fried chicken – their specialty – and loads of chips, or fries in America. The tea was excellent, and the company grand.

A special treat in Ireland is Irish Soda bread. There's nothing quite like it. That's partly due to the flour. My friend Sonia, one of those many culinary school grads, is known for her soda bread. At one point she was making it every day, sending her children off to school with sandwiches made with fresh bread. I had bread at our friend Gen's home and asked for the recipe. She told me it was Sonia's recipe. Sonia agreed to not only share the recipe but teach me how to bake it. I got so good that her own daughter, tasting the bread at my house, thought her mother had made it for me. For my costume at a party I wore an apron with a badge stating "Sonia's student" and carried my partially used Odlums Wholemeal flour bag. The flour is unlike anything available in the US It's coarse, chunky, and littered with wheaty bits. After my return home and a fruitless search for truly coarse flour Wild Flour Bakery in Freestone gave me the number of one of their suppliers. But even at a commercial level there was nothing like the sample I had. You will have to go to Ireland and hope someone as talented as Sonia is the baker where you have the bread.

Sonia also does astonishing theme cakes. They take hours and hours of preparation, imagination, and inspiration. My favorite was the wedding cake shaped like a stack of birch tree rounds surrounded by Snowdrops, moss, ferns, and other flowers.

Plan B: Dr J and Ms S just emailed. They've tired of the rebuilding process. He's taking a job several states away starting January 1. No renewal of obscenely large rent. We're going home just in time for the Xmas travel rush.

On our way to Nenagh, our home for the next month, we stop at the Swiss Cottage, a more than two hundred-year old thatched roof beauty of an ornamental cottage in a wooded setting, with an Irish-green lawn and an 800-year old yew tree shading one side of the mullion-windowed house filled with architectural beauty. It was the fashion for the gentry to create a place where they could pretend to be peasants. Think Marie Antoinette and her little village. They did a wonderful job making a lovely place where no one lived. The owners only visited for a day at a time, bringing their friends along for tea and company. Money has the advantage of paying for quality work that endures. Part of me was saddened by the waste of a two-story playhouse for grown-ups, while another part was taken in by the beauty of it all. The docent, perhaps sensing this or because many feel this way, reminded us that wherever we live we have comforts the crazy rich of that era could only dream of: indoor plumbing and electricity to name just two.

We also stopped in Tipperary proper for an Irish meal at Brazil's. And yes, we hummed "It's a long way to Tipperary" as we walked along the streets.

Nenagh is larger than Fermoy, more city-like. Fermoy is three streets paralleling the Blackwater River and one large street crossing the bridge with smaller streets and estates spidering off the main throughways. Faber Castel, the maker of all those No. 2 pencils, was at home here until recently. A giant pencil marks the intersection across the Blackwater River.

Nenagh's skyline is spiked with a round castle keep. This midland portion of Ireland seems to be both flatter and steeper. Large wide pastures are full of grain or are newly harvested. Steep valleys lead up and up.

Our home for a month is an aging mock Moorish castle about ten minutes outside of town overlooking one of these steep valleys. It's impressive when viewed from across the valley. No doubt, there were some objections as it was being built, but here it is, an inconsistency, an anomaly set amongst the farmhouses and homesteads. It's been empty a while, which has led me to understand that the dust I vacuum and wipe away weekly at home is partly the house itself. When you leave a house unattended it weeps bits of itself into the emptiness. A swift cleaning and things feel immensely better.

And our new location provides another learning curve. The owner, someone we've neither met nor spoken to, took out the televisions and cable box to put a halt to the tv license charged by the government. This is a phenomenon we don't deal with in the US yet is common in Europe. A tv tax pays for the wealth of broadcasting that we in the US love to watch on our local Public Television stations. Evidently, they charge you as long as you have a tv, even if you live out of the country and the house is empty. So we are learning to use my Android as a hotspot in the house, or to settle in to the Abbey Hotel bar for lunch and free WiFi to download ever so slowly some Netflix content, and generally to do without constant access to electronic stimulation of the "What has happened in the world today?" variety. The Abbey Court food is good and the servers are tolerant of our long stays.

Our entertainment one afternoon at home was to watch the farmer down the hill from us herding his cattle. Cows have a surprisingly large vocabulary and in every herd it seems there is an especially vocal one. There's no problem understanding that there is unhappiness in the herd. The farmer in his small tractor with a cattle dog dashing beside him attempted to herd about thirty cows around a clump of trees and down to the next field which lies out of sight beyond the curve of the valley. Cows can be stubborn it seems. Two black ones simply stood where they were and did not participate in the process. A red cow and a black cow took off in the opposite direction. The rest of the herd went complaining down the lane and around the trees. This wasn't what the farmer wanted. He circled them in his tractor, got out, ordered the dog into herding maneuvers, which eventually worked. It wasn't as smooth a process as we imagined based on watching it done on tv. Several options presented themselves: the farmer is new to the work; he's training the dog; or cows are difficult creatures. I think number three must be factored into whatever is going on. We look forward to any repeat performances that might enlighten us, or to running into the farmer at the local P. Kennedy's pub just down the road.

When we first saw P. Kennedy on the side of the house, we thought that was just what it was. A house that had formerly been part of some larger establishment and the name was left behind as a quaint curiosity. We drove by a couple of nights later and wondered if they were having the family over for a meal as there were several cars parked in front. The next day we spotted a car for an environmental service pulled up in front. Husband pulled over and went to knock on the door. It is indeed a pub, not a home. "Come back this evening!" was the happy invitation.

We've been there twice and been introduced to the country pub. Anne, the publican, is friendly in the way of businesspeople everywhere. But the usual Irish welcome is missing from fellow patrons. It felt as if we had interrupted a private party even though it was a half dozen young construction workers clustered on stools at the bar talking sports and work. We settled into a corner; the same one we would go to when we returned with a friend. The Guinness was well poured, and that's the important thing. As to why the reception here was not the happy inclusivity we had felt elsewhere our friend Mike shrugged and said "It's a country pub. People have to get to know you in a small place." Apparently much of the population surrounding the pub is made up of Kennedys.

The reason Mike was with us at P. Kennedy's pub our second time there is that our phones, unbeknownst to us, weren't working. Friends in Fermoy had tried to reach us for two days with no answer from us. So Mike popped an overnight bag in the boot and drove on over. Just a little over an hour to be sure we were alright. He spent the night and went with us the next day to deal with the phones. Something about the move to Nenagh and something not getting properly toggled in the Vodafone system was fixed and we're back in contact with the world again. More on Vodafone later.

It turns out Mike plays 45, a card game that it seemed only my family and my parent's friends played. Five cards to each player, a kitty, bidding, then a suit declared. Black is backward and red is right. If this makes sense to you, then you know the game, too. His rules are a bit different from what I learned, but we could play without a steep learning curve at our table in the back of the pub.

In the Hibernian Inn downtown we had settled in at the restaurant and made our orders when I looked up to see a photograph of the 1916 group. There are ways to determine a local's allegiance. Seeing a photo of the leaders of the 1916 Irish uprising against the British is one indicator. A street named De Valera is another. While you don't have to go far to find Brits who have moved to Ireland there is still the possibility of ill will. We have made friends on both sides of that line. One English woman who has lived in Ireland for thirty years says that it is much better than it used to be, but she is still very aware of prejudice at times.

We have been surprised to have Irish acquaintances turn to us, eyes rolling at something said or done, and say something like, "Well, he is Brit," as though that explains all. We're American, and generally favored and treated quite well, though we are teased about American foibles. It is assumed we live in a large house, have loads of money, and can't tolerate less than the best. We're expected to be loud and proud, so that even when we're being quiet, a fairly normal state for the two of us, it's expected that we'll start in on the loud and proud bit any moment, that we're just holding back.

In Nenagh, a portion of one of the floors of the local museum is given over to the history of the Kennedy clan, including John F. and Robert F. Kennedy. Remember the P. Kennedy pub? This is the homeland of Ireland's most favored American president. More Irish live in America than live in Ireland and Ireland still hasn't reached the population level it was before the Famine of the 1840s. It could be argued that no other country has had such an impact on America. They are one of the national groups to have felt prejudice and moved beyond it. There are no longer "Irish Need Not Apply "or "Irish Not Welcome" signs in the windows of American businesses, just as Swedes are no longer called "blockheads." In the "Peanuts" comic strip "Blockhead!" was a frequently used term of derision that was rooted in anti-Swedish prejudice that has faded away, the meaning of the insult so lost that it's used to entertain children.

In an office on the ground floor of the museum is a genealogist who is paid by the county to help folks search their history. Much of her material, church records and county records, is limited to the county of Tipperary. Even though we don't know the origins of either of our families she helped us with some details. Husband's father's first name led her to believe there was some English sympathy, but then his grandmother's name evoked pure Irish sentiment. She also confirmed that my maiden name is Irish, though shared with England. If we can confirm that either of husband's grandparents went to the US from Ireland, we have a stab at getting Irish citizenship. My great-grandparents were the immigrants, so I don't qualify.

We came to Ireland to enjoy a cool Irish summer. The European heat wave of 2018 altered that. But now, with September barely started we feel winter creeping in. The nights are cool, verging on cold. Bring your coat when you leave the house. We've had fires several nights. The days are cool and a bit humid. Rain showers are no cause for excitement as they would be at home. Wine country in California has very compartmentalized weather. Summers are hot and dry. Fall is warm and dry. Winters are, we hope, wet. Spring is cool and beautiful with a few showers possible. It's the hot and dry part, so good for grapes, olives, and lavender, I'm always trying to circumvent.

Many times I've said I would be happy if summer was only about two weeks long. This summer we got six weeks of it and I find myself disconcerted and unsettled by the swiftness of its passing. In this brief summer I have vacillated between loving the amazing green views and the peace, then feeling claustrophobic driving down the tunnels of green coming on blind curves on narrow roads. The claustrophobia leads to homesickness for a more wide open view. A young German couple who moved to Nenagh a couple of years ago quickly agreed that the state of the roads was sometimes frightening. Esther said she liked the more natural feel of the barely tended Irish roadsides. At home in Germany, she said, the trees would be well trimmed to avoid any possibility of a branch dropping on a car. Everything would be neatly manicured. And then there was a pause and I understood it immediately. While we can love the thing we're in the midst of, the beautiful green wildness, we can miss the different beauty of home. That is a sign of good mental health, the ability to hold two disparate concepts in the mind at once without imploding or exploding. It is also the dilemma of being a traveler. We are glad to be away from the impediments of home, glad to be exploring and experiencing, and at the same moment we miss the surety of home, and the comfort of knowing all there is to know about home.

Travel is closely related to the word travail. "Painfully difficult or burdensome toil; the pain of childbirth." Yeah, I get that.

One day we were eager to see more of the western side of Ireland and to test our ability to get around without our friend Mike at the wheel. So we took off for the Tarbert Ferry, passing through Limerick. On the way we found a small sign for Knockpatrick Gardens and made a quick turn off the road and found a wonder of a garden, or series of gardens, complete with dog and cat to make us feel at home. The home and property were inherited by the couple who have been gardening here for fifty years.

From the top of the garden you look down over the water to Shannon. The garden is a labor of love for them as they give all profits from visitors to charity. We were invited up to the house for a chat and asked to sign the Visitor's Log, international visitors always being welcome.

The crossing on the Tarbert Ferry was uneventful, though I felt the drama of knowing that off to our left was the Atlantic and the next bit of land that direction would be Newfoundland. Our simple passage across the Shannon estuary led us to Kilrush where we had a solid Irish meal at Kelly's Steak and Seafood House followed by a haircut for husband at Jim's Barbershop where Bruce Springsteen memorabilia was on show as Jim had barbered Bruce Springsteen and one of the Trump sons at the nearby Trump property.

Fed and barbered we were on the road again, husband settled in for the drive home, when another sign directed us to Vandeleur Walled Garden. Serendipity had led us to Knockpatrick Gardens while Vandeleur had been planned. Pacing the 170 hectares of well-tended gardens and mature trees was more than husband and his bothersome ankles could handle after Knockpatrick, so I enjoyed them solo. If you're in the Shannon area and you're either a gardener or a garden lover, go to both places.

We have been keeping up with news from home via newspapers on our tablets. It's been a bit spotty here in the castle without WiFi, but we download at the Abbey Court and read it a day or two late. It's why we understood when we got the email from Dr J. Many people in Sonoma County are struggling with the rebuilding process. Some because their fire insurance wasn't what it could have been, others because of the permitting process, others because finding contractors to take on the rebuilding is proving more difficult than they can handle. The Tubbs fire of 2017 has changed the landscape of Sonoma County in more ways than one.

It has changed the emotional landscape as well. I follow my neighborhood on Nextdoor (nextdoor.com). Regularly there are postings asking something like, 'Does anyone else smell smoke?' or 'Is that smoke over the hill?' Replies range from the frantic, 'Are we ok?' to 'Here's the latest post from the Rincon Valley Fire Department. It's under control' For us, distance has eased the anxiety. Though when we catch the news from home and it includes updates on the various fires burning as summer 2018 nears its end, we say "We could still lose the house. In just one night."

An article in the Press Democrat in late September was about the constant need to be ready to go within a minute or two. The night of the Tubbs fire some people didn't have even that. If their Go! bag had been in the closet by the front door there would not have been enough time to get it. The president of my alma mater burned her bare feet running from the flames. (*From running for our lives to renewal, Press Democrat*). Still, it is good sense to have that bag ready and easy to get on the way out the door.

My friend Kathrine was home in Christchurch, New Zealand for a family visit during the devastating earthquakes in 2011. She now keeps a Go! bag by her bed, one in her car, one ready in the house, and one in a shed outside. She motivated me to create my earthquake preparedness kit, going to stores with me to make sure I completed the list. But I wasn't Go! ready on the night of the fires. Since we weren't evacuated, that wasn't a problem. But when we go home, there will be Go! bags. A flash drive with copies of documents, copies of prescriptions, lists of doctors, insurance agents, and banking information. The same documents are in my phone's Gallery. Money, astronaut blankets, water, underwear, toothbrush and paste, comb, soap leaves, flashlight, phone chargers, and more flash drives with all the backups of pictures and historical family documents will be in the bag. While prepping to sell our house I began scanning all our photos. Tubbs and tenants motivated me to complete it, leaving me with flash drives to share all around the family, to have in the Go! bag, and to take with me.

As we hear from and read about those who lost everything in the fires, it is the things that cannot be replaced that are missed the most. The silver spoon that fed your grandfather as an infant might be a blob of melted metal in the ruins. If you've got a picture of it on a flash drive, it might help ease that loss.

I remember another fire when I was about six. We lived down a country lane with small ranchettes on one side and a large pasture on the other. I don't remember where the fire started, but it came into the pasture and the Sheriff came down the lane telling all of us to be ready to evacuate in a few minutes. My mom handed me a bag and told me to put in it what I wanted and then go to the car. I no longer remember what I put in the bag, but I do remember standing at the end of our gravel driveway, leaning on the stone wall, looking at the smoke filling the sky, clutching my doll to my chest, and while I was frightened and excited I also was certain I had all I needed. It was a good feeling. I wish I could ask my mom what she was doing, what she was gathering as I stood and watched the smoke billow up.

The earthquakes in which all California natives are baptized also teach lessons about preparedness. The 1994 Northridge earthquake happened while husband and I and our two children lived in Capistrano Beach. It shook us awake at 4:30 in the morning and we moved into action. We opened the garage door and moved the car out and listened to the news on the car radio as other neighbors doing the same thing greeted us and we exchanged the news we had. The woman who lived across the street was a transplant from Utah and had never been in an earthquake. We answered her questions, assured her we were probably fine, unless we needed to get to LA in the next few days. Then I remembered the bathtub and excused myself to go fill it. "Why?" she asked. "Water," I replied. "I only have a shower," she cried. "We'll share. Probably won't need it, but don't worry." As soon as possible after an earthquake fill your bathtub and any other containers with water. If the quake is bad enough your water supply may be interrupted or contaminated, and you will be glad of that tub full of water. That and keeping a pair of flip flops inside a gallon Ziplock bag under your bedside table is about as far as I got in earthquake preparedness. (Keeping a pair of shoes under the bedside table means they won't get buried under the bed which could be too difficult to lift nor will they be covered in broken glass from windows shattering.)

Until then my experience with quakes had been either/or. Either you were in a world of hurt, or you were fine, inconvenienced perhaps but having had a taste of earth's power. If the latter was the case, then an earthquake preparedness kit was completely unnecessary. And if it was the former, then the idea that you could truly be prepared for an earthquake devastating enough to topple buildings, cut off water and power, and destroy roads was ridiculous. Often the advice was to store items in a plastic garbage can and keep it just inside your garage. Guess which door is least likely to open if you are near the epicenter of a quake? That huge garage door. So there you will be with a load of items that could help you and you won't be able to get to it. I preferred the 'I'll rummage through the rubble for what I need' preparedness model. Then my New

Zealand friend insisted I had to follow through and get ready. The night the Tubbs fire started I was ready for an earthquake. I was ready to shelter in place. I wasn't ready to run.

When our children were small, we prepared for emergencies by playing a game with our kids. In our backyard, perhaps smelling the bonfires down on Doheny Beach, someone would present a scenario. "Dad's at work. Mom's at the grocery store. We're in school. An earthquake hits. What do we do?" Or San Onofre (San Diego's now defunct nuclear power plant) blows up. Or a fire is coming. Or Dad's home and Mom is at the grocery store again, and they were home. (I worked from home, so they had to get rid of me somehow.) Sometimes for variation we'd let one of the kids be home alone. Mom probably went to the pharmacy for medicine for the kid who was home sick from school.

From this we learned what things were most important to each of us. Daughter's blanket, son's bear, mom's pearls, pictures, and computer. For everyone, our cat Miss Kitt. Poor Dad. Neither of us remember what I was supposed to take for him other than the computer which served us both. We also talked through how it would be possible to get these things out of the house. Hint: pillowcases can be filled with stuff and can carry a cat.

For a long time the Red Wagon featured in these escape scenarios. A kid could get stuff, including a cat in a pillowcase, into the wagon and head down the street. Where to go? We made sure they knew the best route to a friend's house. We made sure everyone knew where to leave notes if someone did leave the property. We talked about the importance of staying in place, and how to decide when staying in place was the worst thing to do. We talked about San Onofre, just across the border from San Clemente. We lived within the siren zone, or death zone as we called it. If San O went, so did we if we were at home. Or school. Or grocery store.

There was an annual test of the emergency siren for San Onofre. Around this time one year the school principal sent out what was to be a reassuring letter that in case of such an emergency our children would be bussed to Santa Ana where we could reunite with them. San Onofre officials would call hospitals, nursing homes, and schools who would then initiate evacuation measures and get the old, the sick, and the young out of the way. Then the siren would sound and the rest of us could make a run for it.

"You're going to bus orphans?" I asked.

She did not understand. I do not think she was supposed to disclose this scenario. The logistics of buses and ambulances collecting at multiple sites within a ten-mile radius of San Onofre would be impossible to coordinate and execute without setting off panic. And the idea of children who had been in the emergency zone being bussed out of the zone without parents, to be sick and die alone made me both furious and horrified. The principal could not see anything but the heroic act of rescuing children from an emergency zone. Perhaps I was less educated than I should have been on the actual radius of exposure since thousands can survive the initial meltdown or blowup and not die immediately or always develop cancer later. Nevertheless, I told her to make a note that in such an emergency the McGrath children would not be on the bus. We instructed them to meet up – they chose a place on school grounds – and get home. Climb the fence, run from the adults, whatever it took. It was an imperfect plan, full of potential for real disaster. So was the school district's plan. Movies have been made showing the chaos of evacuation gridlock. We've watched on tv as it played out in hurricane evacuations. We saw it in the fire evacuations.

Now back in Fermoy, settled in the house we were in for the summer, we feel at home, though not at home. Word has come that my brother has more health complications. This makes the miles between us seem even harder, the time needed to get home even longer.

We started this trip with the idea that we might move to Europe. America is home to much of what is wrong with modern life. The rushing, the achieving, the mindless acquisition of more stuff we have to stuff somewhere, the ignorance of our impact on the world. We wanted a slower pace of life, a simpler life, a more productive, thoughtful life. In some ways we have found that. In other ways we see the complications of modern life are everywhere.

Phones

Cell phone service is never as easy as it could be. Given a few decades cell and internet service will become like the landline service we are all so busy getting rid of. It will be easy to get, relatively inexpensive, and absolutely dependable. You don't pick up a landline handset and say, "No reception. I'll call later." "How many bars do you have?" will be something your gramma asked. Until then cell service, internet service is a hassle. When it works you get to do your banking from the couch, your letter writing while reclined on the lawn, your research while sipping Guinness in the local pub, and your photo sorting anywhere you like. When it doesn't work, oh my.

Cell phone service in Europe, once you've gotten the hang of it, is easier and cheaper than anything in the US of A. In Portugal we walked into a Vodafone store at the train station in Lisbon, bought a 20-euro sim card, plugged it in and were good to go. Unlimited talk and text and 6G data for 28 days with rollover. After the salesman accessed some deep menu item that allowed our US phones to connect with their network, we never had a problem. In Ireland the switchover went well also, with the glitch in Nenagh being the only trouble. New numbers, but still unlimited with 6G of data. Once back home we won't sign up for a two-year plan with Verizon as we have done for decades. We will pay twice what we paid in Europe and get less than half the data, which doesn't roll over. But as monthly customers we will pay about half of what we were paying before our Year on the Road. If Vodafone ever comes to the US, we'll be in line to sign up with them.

Another phone tip. We have a bundled package with Xfinity. Every time I try to cancel the land line because it seems we only get robocalls on it anymore I am told that it will be cheaper to keep the bundle and the land line, instead of buying cable and internet on their own. With only a few months to go in Ireland we discovered that we could have been using that Xfinity bundle to keep in touch for free with friends and family in the US. I toggled something on my cell phone and began getting a ring when anyone called the landline back home. One evening I picked it up in time to answer it. A man who had done work for us the year before was checking to see if we needed him again. No, but what number was he calling? He repeated our home number and asked where we were. Ireland, I said. Consternation and surprise all around. We had a chat about Ireland and Santa Rosa and travel, then said our goodbyes. If you've still got a landline bundled with your cable and internet check to see if you can access the landline on your cell and you can call home for free! Otherwise, WhatsApp is standard and works well for phone, text, and video chats. Since it's free and owned by Facebook, you have to know you are being mined, though it is encrypted.

There are a few other interesting differences between home and Ireland. I remember using Kleenex, or its European version, here somewhere, but mostly it's toilet tissue that's used for noses. You can buy boxes of tissue – there's a small selection offered at some groceries. And if you're out and about and need a tissue a friend will hand you a purse pack from which you will pull a larger-than-US tissue. Otherwise, in homes there are no tissue boxes lurking in the various corners one might expect in the US: bathroom counter, kitchen counter, bedside table. It makes me wonder if we are so attached to our boxes only because of good marketing campaigns by manufacturers who have created another false need. I remember in the US visiting an older friend who had the flu. She had a roll of toilet paper by the couch where she was reclined. I offered to get her some "real" tissue. Her answer was that if it was good enough for her tender parts it was good enough for her nose.

On another note, if you buy a box of raspberries or blackberries in Europe eat them that day or the next. In California I can buy a box of berries and several days later they are still in my fridge looking nearly as good as the day I brought them home. Not so here. I've thrown out more than several tubs of berries because I kept putting off using them. Vegetables spoil faster too. I'm sad to admit that at home sometimes I buy broccoli, put it in the crisper and then forget about it. Rarely have I had to throw out the whole thing. I have had to throw out several heads of broccoli in Portugal and in Ireland. Which makes me suspicious of what is happening to my fruit and veg in California. Why does it last longer there? Genetically modified? Sprayed with some chemical? This tendency to spoil has changed my attitude toward groceries. Now I come home with a plan to use them today or tomorrow. Maybe the day after, but don't count on it. Husband is frustrated with going to the market every two or three days. I remind him that for years he was out of the house working and didn't see how often I went to the market. Hmm. Perhaps my children's disaster stories of "Mom is at the grocery store" begin to make sense.

When I mention the fruit and veg going bad so quickly my Scottish friend who has lived here for thirty years says, "Yes. Everything comes from so far away. Nothing's local anymore." Well, there goes my theory of genetic modification as the culprit. Perhaps.

What makes a simple life is not having too much, whether it's stuff or obligations or needs. Making do makes it easy. Google the question "How many clothes do I need?" and you get a wide variety of answers, all dependent on what you do in life. At home every time I look in my closet, I see that I could get rid of much of what is in there and not miss it. Now I have two suitcases of clothes, a couple of pieces I could have left behind, a couple of pieces I packed away I would be glad to have with me. But I also have learned that I could do with less. If we ask the people we come across regularly they might be of a different opinion. Somewhere someone might be saying, "Is she really wearing that again? Does she have nothing else?" "No," is the answer. And other than a bit of boredom with my selection (but seven months on the road as I write this!) I am certain I could have packed less. Now that summer seems to be over, I am thinking of boxing up what I don't need and shipping it home. Husband has a few things he would like to unload. He's tired of schlepping a suit bag around, but our volunteer work requires suits for him, so he's looking to unload some things he was sure he would need and now doesn't. Husband is also thinking that instead of dragging suitcases home he will ship everything but a carryon home. He is not a happy traveler under the best of circumstances and negotiating four suitcases and a carryon makes him mad with frustration, especially when some young thing zips past with only a backpack. "Probably headed to the beach," I tell him. Packing for Hawaii would be a breeze. Two swimsuits, two shorts, a coverup, a skirt, several tee shirts, a shawl, sandals, a couple of gallon Ziploc bags for the wet suits/shorts. Done. That could all go in a carry-on bag.

When I went back to school for my Master's I had a self-imposed uniform of several pairs of khaki pants, and black tees in varying sleeve lengths, along with a variety of colorful scarves and cardies (cardigans or sweaters – I really am picking up the Irish). It's not all I had, but some variation of this is what I kept happily returning to. Not until I had to work with the public did I alter the uniform, upping my game to business casual and thereafter filling my closet.

If I had the nerve I would do what one woman did, a Rothschild,

I think. She hit about forty and decided she was tired of fashion. She liked gardening and she liked her dogs. She went to the family tailor and designed a roomy dress with pockets for seeds and etc. as well as dog treats. She ordered a set number per year, choosing new fabrics. I'm sure she had other things as well, being a Rothschild has its obligations, but this was her daily wear. I would like to follow her example, but I do not have her nerve, not do I have a big name to excuse my eccentricities.

Once again travel leads to life, just as life leads to travel. If you live you need stuff. If you don't travel you may not realize how little stuff you need. And if you travel you realize that the stuff you have is not necessarily the stuff you need. All I know is I have too much of said stuff and am always struggling with how to get the right amount of stuff and the right kind of stuff. And I don't want so much stuff that I have to find a place to put my stuff because it's too much stuff to live with. (Thank you, George Carlin.) This is a problem only magpies have to deal with in the animal world, and only because they are collectors, too.

"What?"

A frequent question in my home. After the illness in Boliquieme, Portugal that left me deaf in my right ear and not hearing so well out of the left I have recovered, but not completely. At the slightest rise in elevation my ears pop and crackle. I know I'm missing bits of conversation, am aware that I'm filling in the missing bits so that I don't have to keep asking, "What?" It's bad enough to keep doing it to husband, but not to friends or strangers. My Irish doctor recommends another round of antibiotics to clear the liquid from behind the eardrums. We settle on the less chemical route of daily saline rinses, over-the-counter antihistamines, and sinus spray.

Which has made me realize that the conversations I have heard over my lifetime and attributed to the sad state of marriage are in fact quite the opposite. Oh, I know there are long-term marriages where the parties really have come to despise one another but don't have the gumption to battle back to a healthy relationship, nor the will to end it. But in the past several months I have come to a different view of the loudly telegraphic conversations I have heard.

"Salmon!"

"Goat cheese!"

This is not an argument you're hearing. It's not overhearing either since it's at a decibel level that includes nearby tables. This is a very shorthand version of the conversation this same couple might have had years earlier when their hearing was less impaired.

"They have wild salmon, just as you hoped."

"Sweetie, they have a goat cheese appetizer and a goat cheese salad. You love goat cheese."

"Bank!" translates to "I need to stop at the bank to get some cash for the weekend. Don't think there will be many ATMs on the walking trails out there."

"Lettuce!" is actually "Please pick up a good head of lettuce, too while you're at the store."

Try this next time you're out and forced to hear the private back and forth between an older couple near you: fill in the bits you didn't hear. It will be good practice for the day you realize you've said "What?" way too many times that day.

And always keep in mind that hearing loss might not be a couple issue, but yours alone. The classic joke is the husband who goes to his doctor for a checkup and mentions that his wife is losing her hearing, but she won't believe him. The doctor recommends a test the husband can perform at home. The man goes home, steps in the door and seeing his wife in the kitchen at the stove he calls out, "Honey! I'm home! What's for dinner?" No answer. As he expected. He moves further into the house and repeats his lines. No answer again. A third time he moves closer to his wife in the kitchen. No answer. The fourth time he is standing right behind her. She turns to him, cooking spoon in hand. "For the fourth time, it's chicken!"

Always check your perception against reality.

Anniversary

The anniversary of the Tubbs fire has come and gone. Technically. The fire started on October 8, reaching Santa Rosa in only four hours but it burned through the night and kept burning until it merged with other fires, and wasn't put out for weeks. So the anniversary is only the anniversary of that first horrific, mind-bending, life-altering night.

We have followed the stories in the Press Democrat online. *"Fires' anniversary triggers stress"* highlights the long-term effects and the attempts to mitigate them even as the anniversary dredges up the fear and anger.

Developmentally speaking we acquire the idea of object permanence while still in diapers. Before this milestone our toys disappear and are simply gone; no need to cry for or look for them. Once we realize things can be found, that people return, it hurts to lose them and so babies cry when the caregiver leaves, they sob when their favorite toy cannot be found. Our brains mature and we realize that when a loved one goes out of sight we do not have to collapse in a heap of heartrending sobbing. They will return. Then we combine the idea of object permanence with the experience of loss as teddies and blankies and sometimes loved ones are lost despite our hearts aching for them. Later still we let ourselves fall prey again to the illusion of safety and solidity, imagining that now we are the adults we can create a place or a circle of people that can't go missing. Why is it that so many of us have a stash of keys somewhere, keys to locks we no longer have, keys to doors we no longer remember? We keep them because each key is an entry to something we have certainly lost and wish to have back, all the pieces of our past neatly lined up and accounted for.

Those who lost it all in the Tubbs fire, like our tenants, are not now and will never be made whole again. They have each lost irreplaceable things and have lost the sense of certainty that home gives. If husband and I feel this then I know that those who lost it all that night must also feel that nothing can ever be certain again. Every time I lock the door and drive away from the house it is with the knowledge that that home and all that is in it could be gone before I return. And it is also possible that I will never return home. I think of the woman the first night of the fire who drove off the lane she had driven for decades and died. The couples who stayed in their pools for hours as the fire burned around and over them. The people trapped in a parking lot not far from my house who waited it out as the fire burned over them. The family who lost both of their children trying to run from the fire. Those whose loved ones were too incapacitated to get themselves to safety. Those who ran for their lives. Those who, like Linda, my son's mother-in-law, after banging on the doors of the nearest neighbors, drove her neighborhood with horn blaring and lights flashing. Those like another friend, Ralph, who gave their all and saved lives that night only to die himself months later. Those who committed suicide because what they had lost and the impossibility of recreating a semblance of their pre-fire life was too much to bear. Those who looked around after the fire had passed and chose to move on. Those who had nowhere to go and not enough resources to stay, who became homeless in a profound way that night. All of them casualties. Multiply it out to Portugal, Spain, and Greece where wildfires also took lives and homes that summer and fall. Add the losses to fires since then. Imagine the losses behind us and those ahead of us. What an anniversary.

A storm blew through last night. It made its presence felt at the London wedding of Princess Eugenie, blowing hats off royal guests, and roiling the shrubbery. Clouds and wind are still here, everything shining clean and the fresh smell you only get after the storm. Fire has no similar after-effect.

With great effort I try to turn my mind away from the anniversary and towards the life I have now. The question is how to turn away while still keeping it in focus. Life lessons should be kept in plain sight lest they get covered over with the detritus of daily life. The errands, the small things of each day. The lettuce to be washed, dried, torn, bathed in oil and vinegar, then eaten, washed up after, the bowl put away, another meal at the end of another day further away from the memory.

Every good experience in this year on the road is filtered through the reason for our being on the road. Great loss has led to our abundance. I am unable, for now, to fully enjoy where I am because of where I have come from. The fire is with us no matter how far we have traveled.

With our application for a Stamp 0 visa we now have permission to stay longer while we await the decision. But we cannot leave Ireland. We haven't seen nearly enough of Ireland. We are focused on our town and its surrounding villages and the people we have befriended here. Our trips are mainly day trips. But knowing that if I leave the country to go to Belfast or London or catch that 29-euro flight to Paris I cannot return makes me itch to go. Husband is happy to be settled, as am I in my own way. But I am glad to be settled so that I have a base to fly from. And I cannot fly. My 90 days is up. I can leave but I cannot return. I try to imagine if that was my permanent status, like immigrants who have come across a border illegally and no matter what has happened at home, they know that if they leave, they will probably never return to their illegal haven.

Our status is no real comparison.

In a world without borders, like oil and water, people would gravitate to where they wanted to be. It is an illusion Americans have, that everyone wants to be there. Most people want to stay near their home. Most people would be happy to go back where they came from if there were work and food and safety. Refugees usually come to make a living without fear of getting shot at, tortured or blown up. And the reason many choose somewhere in Europe is both proximity and the fear we have heard so many times – that if they went to America, if they got in, they'd be shot. Because everyone has guns, don't they? We assure them that's not true, but they don't believe us. And it's not hard to see why. We tell them most guns are owned by a minority of people, and most of those people don't carry them around as in the Westerns on tv. If you stay out of gang territory you're probably as safe as anywhere in Europe. Heads shake. Denial. I'm a privileged white woman, so what do I know.

Soon after one of these discussions about guns I read an account in the Press Democrat about a criminal who got away from police, then was fired on by an armed bystander. He missed. No action was taken against the shooter because he lived in an open carry state. No mention was made of what happened to the stray bullet fired by the armed bystander. I must refine my answer to potential visitors to the US of A about safety from guns to include open carry information.

My husband, raised by women who hunted to feed the family, is a respecter of guns, and a hunter who hasn't hunted in years. Guns are, to him, useful tools, admirable mechanical creations. We do not share this predilection. However, even he was taken aback in the first stages of our Year On the Road by a man at the Grants Pass, Oregon car wash, who stood watching his car get washed with his holstered gun on his hip. My husband, who knows and appreciates guns, did not feel safer. I did not feel safer when he told me about it. At least when a policeman has a gun we can hope that he or she has been properly trained in their use, and in de-escalation techniques. Of course, we know that's not always true, hence the headlines and the fear. But a guy wearing his gun in public because he can...well, I'm sorry, but the only correlation I can make is to a flasher, the guy in the overcoat who wants you, really wants you, to look at his equipment and be impressed, or afraid, or attracted. So if every person who wanted to carry their gun in public also had to wear a shifty-looking trench coat we would at least be warned. We wouldn't know what they were packing, but we'd be warned.

Our Stamp O visa has been approved. We have permission to stay until October 2019. But we must return to Santa Rosa in January because Dr J and Ms S will have moved. Our permission to stay and our intention to stay do not match the necessity to leave. Such is life. And for this we have paid about 1,000 euros. From the certified Irish accountant to the actual cost of the visas. This does not count the over 200 euros monthly for Irish health insurance which we cannot use for the first six months. Immigration is a nice little profit-maker for a country.

Camp Fire

As I write this one year and one month after the Tubbs fire started, we are waiting for news on husband's sister's house in Paradise, California. The Camp Fire began Thursday, November 18, 2018 and in one day grew to 70,000 acres. Minor injuries, no deaths reported so far, just acres of loss, and loss and loss. Homes, businesses, memories. Husband spent some formative years in Paradise, down a steep canyon shaded by massive trees that ended in the Little Butte Creek where great times were had in the hot summers at Little Pearl and Big Pearl. There he found the solitude to begin to find his footing to deal with the death of his big brother and the breakup of his parent's marriage. Gramma lived on the other side of the lane down the canyon. To think of those places being gone to him is achingly difficult. It's hard to take a deep breath here remembering how it is with the smoke in the air, the ash falling so quietly, all the while wondering what's left, what's left.

Husband's sister was out of town when the fire started, so she has only what she had with her. She was the keeper of mementos and papers and the stuff that gets left behind when a loved one dies. We wait to know if it is gone. We want to hope that no one died in this conflagration but know it is a futile hope. This monster will have killed people. We cringe at what is ahead for the people who have been burned out. The emotional toll, the physical toll, the mind-numbing and spirit crushing battle of the insurance claim and the rebuilding.

A friend just texted to say Malibu and Westlake Village in Southern California are under mandatory evacuations. Husband's twelve-string guitar is being cared for by a friend very nearby there. I'm going to have a piece of chocolate and a glass of port. Good night.

Good news and bad news for us. Good news is that sister-in-law's house was not burned down. Hers is one of three down the canyon that survived. At this writing the area is still under mandatory evacuation orders and no one is allowed in. A fireman neighbor sent a brief video showing the house still standing but looking as though it may have been looted. Why her house survived is a mystery.

The other good news is that the friend caring for the twelve-string arrived home from Santa Rosa (where he is still coordinating with fire victims, their insurance companies, and the Planning Department) to find that his wife and daughters had packed the cars for evacuation. The fire came within one-quarter mile of their home. They are safe and so is the guitar.

The bad news is that at this moment 88 are confirmed dead (85 as of September 2019) in the Camp Fire, and Paradise seems to be lost. We wonder if it might not have been better for the house to have burned because there will not be a town nor a community. The canyon is steep and with only three homes in it will be immensely lonely. It will be more like it was when the gold miner built his cabin across the lane in 1850. Quiet and lonely. And for her perhaps not safe.

Today I was on a quick trip with local friends. We stopped for fuel and the driver only put in a few euros worth. When I remarked that it was a quick fill-up, he said that they don't fill up, just put in what you've got in your pocket at the moment. I told them that in California we are told to always keep a half tank of gas in our cars. They thought I meant that gas was so cheap that we might as well keep it nearly full. No, I told them. It's in case of fire. Half a tank is as good as empty. You don't want to run out of gas when you're running from flames. And in case of earthquake the electricity might be off, and you can't pump gas without electricity. Then I told them about filling the bathtub with water after a quake. After a bit of a silence Martin said, "You always think the grass is greener until you get to know it." True. The disasters in Irish history have been famine, war, and revolt. These are no more able to be effectively planned for than our series of natural disasters. I looked out the window as we whizzed along the narrow road at a Mr. Toad's Wild Ride pace and though the grass is truly green here, I ached for home.

Driving

The first few times behind the wheel on the "wrong" side of the car and zipping along on the "wrong" side of the road are enervating. It doesn't take long before it's rare for one or the other of us to shout "Irish side!" when we stray to the American side of the road. That we don't shout "Wrong side!" is much appreciated by our friends, along with our switching sides quickly. While making a left turn takes a while for me to get, left-handed shifting comes easier than I expected.

A common dilemma for drivers almost everywhere is the traffic jam. In Cork and Dublin we had a few moments of that. On the rural roads the jams are of another much more enjoyable nature. Livestock needs to be moved from pasture to pasture. Sometimes this involves getting on the road. We have sat a few times waiting for a group of nervous cows to get by our car. Note: turn off the engine for them. The sheep seemed not to care if the car was off or on, they just wanted to get past. We saw animals herded by tractors, by vehicles, and a couple of times by a cycling farmer.

Now that husband and I are more accustomed to driving the narrow, winding, blind curves of Irish roads I will put on the radio if I'm driving a familiar route. A radio station in Cork sometimes has American announcers. It's jolting to hear that accent coming from my Irish radio. When I listen to the talk shows there is always lots of talk in rolling, lilting, and occasionally nearly unintelligible accents. The subjects are sometimes over my head, and the dangers of concentrating on Irish politics or health care while driving are very real to me. So I turn to music.

I am not musically literate enough to know why I have never been able to listen to the blues without feeling blue or why country music just causes instant depression. In Irish music I hear something like a country beat, but with something added, and I like it. Or is this like my newfound tolerance for spicy food? Neither my aging taste buds nor my brain are so reactive, perhaps.

Recently I came across the song of the summer here in Ireland. Now we're in autumn it's about time I found the summer song. It's "Shotgun" by George Ezra. How odd it is to hear a British accent (sorry Ireland) giving a twang to words that might come from a country song but swing back into something else not quite English, but not American. It's an interesting experience.

Mudlarking

A group of us made a trip to Galway where we indulged in a new hobby. Mudlarking. If you've not heard of it, start with *tidelineart.com,* or check it on YouTube. Mudlarking used to be the purview of the poor scrabbling in the riverside mud for anything that could be used or sold. Now it's the province of those who qualify with the Port of London Authority to search for treasure in the leavings of the Thames as the tide uncovers things tossed yesterday and those tossed millennia ago. Anything of potentially historical importance – like Roman artifacts – must be handed over to be catalogued. If pieces in better condition already exist, the finder may get it back. It's a badge of honor to have a find on display in a museum.

While in Galway we indulged ourselves. No permit needed as mudlarking hasn't gotten there yet. The River Corrib which runs through Galway is a tidal river as the Thames in London is. This means there are daily surges to cover and uncover treasure. We were unprepared for mudlarking. We only thought of it as we stood outside the Galway City Museum and contemplated the river. Then we decided to go for it, causing locals to stare at us until one man finally called down, "What are ye doing there?" Later a woman who watched it all said she had heard of mudlarking, but hadn't thought of doing it here, but now she was going to try. We found bits of pottery, a bowl of an 18th or 19th century tobacco pipe, lovely beach glass, and other interesting things.

When we went to Galway we saw the change in landscape from cattle country, rich and lush with grass, to sheep country, still green and lush but interspersed with rocks large and small. The wind honed the landscape and sculpted trees in ways a bonsai master would appreciate. For eons farmers have pulled the abundant rocks from the ground and made fences and houses. The fences run and run and run, a seemingly endless supply of rocks to make them taller or longer. We saw amongst this rocky sheep-scattered landscape the bogs from which turf is cut. We saw the turf stacks next to the latest cuts, then saw the curves of turf on sale at local markets.

We were able to see the bog as it is before the cut because Ballylanders Gun Club in County Limerick has built walkways and trails so you can get out into Griston Bog without becoming part of the bog. Schoolchildren are brought here to see the geographical history of their homeland. Walking out into it feels like stepping into something living, much like stepping into a redwood grove feels like stepping into a community of living creatures. It is as if the pull of gravity is stronger here. In minutes the sky goes from grey and rainy to bright sunshine with blue sky and then a swift moving bank of fog rolls in completely obscuring the bowl of mountains curving beyond the bog. It is a treasure of a place, a still and quiet place full of life.

We've been to Galway, Clifden, Tralee in County Kerry, Dunquin on the Dingle Peninsula, Dublin, Cork, along with numerous sites close enough to Fermoy to be day trips. Each has been unique, a pleasure in its own right. Since Ireland is about half the size of California, I find myself surprised that there are so very many places to go within such a small space. When our new Irish friends come to visit, we will be hard pressed to take them for a drive of an hour or two and show them as many amazing things as they have shown us. We have redwood trees, Fort Ross, San Francisco, the coast with all of its precious spots. It won't add up. They'll be able to feel smug as we show them our oldest sites that are only a couple of hundred years old, while just the other day I drove over a bridge built in 1436. It's still in use, hasn't been rebuilt, and qualifies as the oldest continuously used bridge in Europe. And in a few minutes drive from downtown Fermoy we can wander in a dolmen, a megalithic tomb. All over Ireland we come across dolmens and standing stones. Often the standing stones are near or in a cemetery.

Near one cemetery we found an interesting sign notifying that unapproved persons should not try to dig graves as it is a dangerous activity. We could get a list of approved grave diggers via a website. And we were to take notice that the local authorities accepted no liability for injuries sustained while digging a grave, even those voluntarily digging a grave. This left us with all kinds of questions. Digging a grave to put someone in? Or digging up a grave? Would the authorities accept liability if the grave digger was not doing so voluntarily? And under what circumstance would one be digging a grave without having volunteered to do so? This particular cemetery had burials dating back to the 7th century further complicating the questions in our minds.

Another happy trip was to Dunquin, a tiny spot on the end of the Dingle Peninsula. Dingle itself is a quaint town on a lovely harbor where Fungi the famous dolphin can be found. We didn't see him on our harbor walk, but we weren't long in the town itself as we had reserved a cottage near the Blasket Island Centre, which is on the mainland, not the island.

Blasket Island can be visited via a regular boat. We didn't. We were enamored of the cottage and the beauty of the peninsula and chose to stay close by. The weather lent itself to walking, so we did. The island was the home of a village of native Irish speakers that became the source of language studies. The day we were at the Centre there was an annual meeting of Irish speakers. While there was a loud American holding forth with her British friends, most people were speaking in Irish. The loud American was not being loud by American standards, but we have noticed that Americans are louder than just about everyone except overserved pub patrons. I attribute it to years of teachers telling us, "Speak up!"

Inside the Centre in a photo exhibit of what had been left behind on Blasket when it was abandoned was a photograph showing a home's interior with a picture of JFK and Jackie on the wall. Because we had just been in Nenagh we understood somewhat the fascination with the Kennedys. We had heard that from the 1960s on many Irish homes had hung a picture of JFK next to the pope.

Ballyferriter, the next village over from Dunquin, proudly displays its connection to the Star Wars movie filmed near here. Take your picture with Darth or Yoda on the sidewalk with the opening words, in Irish, scrolling up the front of Tigh Ui Chathain, a restaurant and B&B. Inside, after a good meal, we met a couple of travelers who live down the road from our old place in Capistrano Beach. We reminisced about home and shared tips about the Peninsula, amazed again at how few degrees of separation there are between us all. We ate delicious food in Murphy's across the road another night so go there, too.

"Ryan's Daughter" (1970) was filmed in this area. Our landlord left the DVD in the player and we watched it our first night. There are several movie locations still around which we spotted as we drove around the peninsula to see a pottery shop and have tea. Inch Strand, the long, long beach of the movie is right here, the location of the army camp still visible, but disassembled.

There's a reason that movies were made here. It's a beautifully wild, open, free place, reminding both of us of the northern California coast.

In this far west side of Ireland you will find that signs, monuments, and menus are often Celtic only, English not always on offer. We were grateful to whoever plastered "Dublin" on the road sign we came to as we were leaving for Fermoy.

A friend had loaned husband "An Unsung Hero," the story of Tom Crean (pronounced Crane) and his treks to the Antarctic with Shackleton and Scott. He gets short shrift outside of this book, even though both expedition leaders give him credit as a lifesaver. Tom retired to the village of Annascaul and opened a pub he named the South Pole Inn. On our way home from the Dingle Peninsula we made a pilgrimage there and were rewarded with a fantastic riverside location, loads of memorabilia inside, and, according to husband, the best seafood chowder ever. My goat cheese salad was right up on top of the list of bests as well. After we were back in Fermoy we came upon a documentary about the Shackleton treks. One brief mention of Tom Crean is all there was. More anti-Irish sentiment? Or just not enough time in the documentary to tell the full story? Depends on who you ask.

By the time we leave Ireland we will have been here for the longest day of the year and the shortest day of the year. Though it isn't a full year, we arrived in spring, will have stayed through summer and fall, then part of winter. Friends have been reminding me that during the unusually warm summer I kept asking when we'd see rain. There has been plenty of it lately. Lots of rain. Lots and lots.

In 2017 Ophelia came through bringing hurricane strength winds, uprooting thousands of trees, and bringing a new benchmark for Irish storms. So far this year none are as bad as Ophelia.

November 28 we met Diana, as in the storm named Diana. As for the arrival of a princess there was lots of preparation, warnings, and anticipation. Then she came through in a whirlwind and left chaos behind.

December 15 Deirdre settled in. As with Diana there has been anticipation and preparation. The gusting winds, the torrential downpour, the water running down the roads are all reminders we are living in a changing climate.

A few days later another storm came through, an unnamed storm, but stronger here than Deirdre had been. Wind was so strong it made us afraid the windows would cave in. But no. We're in a solid Irish home. I slept fine. Husband unwillingly kept track of the storm's progress by tossing and turning until the early hours.

Husband went to the Heron Cafe to have coffee with friends as he often does on a Monday morning. While there a film crew came in for a cuppa. He got to chatting with them and ended up being interviewed because of our Tubbs fire and Camp fire connections. Virgin TV is to carry it. The producer has already been on to him to see if he can get a follow-up interview via Skype when we're home.

The crew were in town to highlight the award Fermoy has been given as the Cleanest Town in Ireland. The next day we had an open-air tea break at the Glanworth Mill at the site of Europe's oldest bridge still in use. An Englishwoman visiting there on her way to shopping in Fermoy has lived in Ireland fifty years. Now she's in Waterford, former home of the crystal factory. She prefers to drive to Fermoy for the shopping. "They're more upscale," she says. The award and the chance meeting with this woman made me look around a bit differently today as I made my way through town.

Fermoy has been here for hundreds of years, as most towns and villages have been. Built long before cars and lorries and massive farm tractors the roads are narrow, sometimes quite twisty or steep. Tractors enormous and small are part of the local street traffic. How did horses pull carts up these steep hills? My car, old beast that it is, has a hard enough time.

Fermoy is not a thatched roof village by a serene lake or gently flowing river. Right now the flood gates are up all along the town and at the bridge. The Blackwater River is right up to the banks and in the last storm came up to the edge of the riverside street. The gates were in place and kept the river on its side of things. The river is lovely to look at, attracting herons, gulls, salmon, fishermen and scullers. A sculling competition is one of the summer highlights. Fermoy is a working town. Computer firms and world class agricultural research as well as a technical college keep it humming. The main street through town is lined with two and three- story buildings of varying ages. A wall on the river side of the street dates back to the abbey that pre-dates the settlement of the town itself. The Great Recession of 2008 did a number on a country that had been a Celtic Tiger and is now more of a Celtic Wildcat. Some Fermoy shopfronts are empty. Places are for sale and have been and will be for some time.

A change in the drink driving standards also did a number on village pubs. One pint can put you over the limit here if you try to drive in less than an hour. The small pubs are disappearing. We've driven through many tiny villages with a boarded-up pub and no apparent gathering spot for the locals. I'm all for getting drunks out from behind the wheel, but I also wonder at the social implications of removing so many places where people got together for a craik (conversation) and a pint away from the isolation of the farm.

On our way to the Dingle Peninsula we were pulled over on the M8, a freeway, by a police officer waving us from the side of the road into an inspection line. License, car registration, questions about where you are going, where you have been. The inevitable follow-up question to Americans, especially those driving a ten-year old car: "What are you doing here?" As the officer was about to wave us away I asked why there was a checkpoint.

"Drink drivers," he said.

"It's noon!" I said.

"Right," he said.

Well, it makes me think that the police back home should rethink their timing, because if you can catch a drink driver at noon you're catching a serious drunk. The couple coming home after a leisurely dinner and a couple of glasses of wine aren't the ones you really want.

Irish history is full of the treachery of men seeking power over others. That never works out, but they keep at it. Brexit has brought a surfeit of news coverage, but no one quite knows what will happen if and when it happens. Amongst our Irish friends we have men and women who were

IRA, British Army, and Irish Army. All are anxious because there is a resurgence of all varieties of Irish nationalism. None of them want to go back to the Troubles. It's hard to imagine it could happen, but Bloody Sunday of 1972 is in the memory of living people.

At a local café sharing pots of tea and scones someone asked what I thought of the British/Irish conundrum. As sometimes happens in a noisy environment there was a pause when all was momentarily quiet except for my reply, something prejudiced and badly informed.

Later in the week the friend who is former IRA and the friend who is former Irish Army were at our house for dinner. Husband said that I was probably on someone's watchlist for my public comment. "No," one of them replied. "But you might get a free coffee."

The anxiety is real. This same friend has taken us to rural areas and told us to be careful what we say as we tour the graveyards or historical sites. Why? Because he has taken us to areas where extended families live quietly and are suspicious of visitors. Bold, loud Americans with a confidence in the guarantee of freedom of speech can make trouble or get in trouble. We hope he is being overly cautious, and then we wonder.

When he went to Northern Ireland for his daughter's wedding to a man from the North the groom's family asked them not to speak in certain places. Their accent would identify them as being from County Cork and there are neighborhoods in the North where that is not a good thing. It was the same when the groom's family visited the bride's family near Cork. Caution is the wisest course.

Shortly before we're due to leave for home a car blows up in Londonderry. The next day we ask friends what it means. It was a message, they say, to the British who were about to have a vote on something to do with Brexit. The question of a hard border in Ireland is a complicated and thorny issue. Londonderry is only called that by the British. Irish call it Derry. The explosion that blew up the car caused no damage to anyone or anything else. It is presumed that the neighborhood had been warned away. We realize how thin is the skin of peace.

Brexit moves on like a landslide in slow motion. Husband and I will be home by the time it actually happens, watching on the nightly news, hoping that the transition will not endanger our friends.

The Tubbs fire put us on the road and the Camp fire is bringing us home.

Trying to manage sister-in-law's needs from Ireland is making a difficult process even harder. She needs help. Her home is still standing but damaged. Insurance will clean and restore and reimburse. But since PG&E has removed the electric meter there is no telling when she will be able to live in her home again. After a month she was able to return for fifteen minutes under Sheriff escort. She called and told us that living there would be like living in an ash can, nothing but destruction and reminders of loss all around her. She, like many in Sonoma County, may choose not to return. This combined with the departure of our lovely tenants has led us to settle return travel arrangements.

We need a one-way ticket home. Since we do not know what awaits us, or how long it will take to settle things regarding our house and sister-in-law's house we can't predict a return date. It might not happen. But airline booking is crazy enough that it is cheaper to buy a round-trip ticket and not use the second half than it is to buy the one-way ticket. We have an opportunity to attend a convention in Germany in the summer, so I booked a flight to Germany not knowing if I would actually be able to use it, but knowing that even if I didn't, I would still have saved money. It feels like a game with tedious formulas and trickery, a game to which I don't know the rules. By the time I click "Book It!" I'm exhausted, frustrated, and certain I've missed a better deal. I do not have good feelings towards the company that will be in charge of providing me a safe and uneventful flight. If I followed my own advice this would take less than an hour because I would not waffle, but just make the decision.

I digress. Again. I wish to be a grateful person. I have a home to return to, to worry about. I have the money to book the flight. I have the freedom to consider returning to Ireland, to a convention in Germany, or staying contentedly in one of the earth's most beautiful spots, Sonoma County. How quickly I vacillate between whining and gratitude.

Now that the tickets are purchased, I find myself making plans for settling in at home. We sold much of our furniture. We don't know if we'll be able to sell our home, or if a down market will mean we stay put for a while. Before we headed to Europe we had considered full-time RVing in the States. We haven't completely abandoned that idea. Acquiring another houseful of furniture is counter-productive to the less encumbered life we both have enjoyed in the last year, knowing also that we are less encumbered because we're renting someone else's stuff. But we will need somewhere to sit and to sleep. Between Ikea and Nextdoor deals I hope to find a couch, perhaps a dining table, and beds, plural. Irish friends would like to visit and as long as we have a house, we'll be glad to put them up and show them around.

With my mind split between thinking of my last few weeks in Ireland and what needs to be done at home, and the options we have to choose from I flip between excitement, dread, and regret. Glad we have done this year, excitement at going home to family and friends, dread at the amount of work this all will be and regret for all I've left undone here. I am remembering all these places, and all those I've not written about like Ross Castle near Killarney, Torc Waterfall, Black Valley, Doneraile Court, Cork City, and the museums and beauty of Dublin. Travel reminds us that the world is much larger than we can ever manage to see. This great blue marble in the vast dark universe is too large for even a lifetime project.

> "Travel makes one modest. You see what a tiny place you occupy in the world."
>
> Gustave Flaubert, French novelist

Mail

Our address in Fermoy was our names, the neighborhood name, the city and county, and a 7-digit alphanumeric code that identified our house. We were told the post could get something to us with just the 7-digit code and either the city or county name. We did not test that theory. The 7-digit code is called an EIR (pronounced "air") code. Type that number into Google and you'll get a map to the location.

One day we got a package for the father of our landlord showing a commercial address connected to the father. But the postman knew the package would get to dad via the tenants in the son's house. Ingenious and correct. When we phoned to tell him what we had received he was not surprised. "Oh, these mailmen are quite good. They know everything."

Packages mailed from us to the US and from the US to Ireland have all arrived in good nick, including the small box I found on the bathroom floor. The postman had chucked it through the slightly open window to keep it from getting wet in the rain. No harm done as it was well wrapped and it missed the toilet. Husband and I, assured of the superior service of the Irish Post, have decided to pack a couple of boxes and ship them home. Shipping a box is about the same price as flying with a second piece of luggage and shipping will free us up in the airport. Though I would have said I didn't buy much while here people have given us mementos, and I bought a couple of T shirts, a sweater, a pair of summer shoes, and a pullover. There is no trouble with leaving behind a few things at the local charity shop (aka: thrift store), so I will be able to get the suitcase closed. We will each take our empty suitcase and put it inside our other suitcase, and then pack the inner suitcase, a tricky way to get both suitcases home.

Husband will carefully carry home by hand a roll of pictures we acquired from our friends Ken and Mary. Their clan has been especially kind to us in navigating our stay. Ken is a talented artist, though he denies it. After we discovered his skill others told us where we could find his work hanging around town. He opened his archives to us and is sending us home with special mementos of places we saw and those we wish we had seen.

The box we send off to my brother's house – just in case it arrives before I'm home to receive it - is seventeen kilograms or 37.48 pounds of summer clothes and shoes, a few souvenirs, and the raincoat husband packed and never wore. That's one suitcase we don't have to battle with on the way home. Husband will ship a second one after I leave for London and then each of us have only one suitcase to deal with in airports, shuttles, etc.

Waiting at home for me will be a box of things I thought enough of to ship home. When I face the boxes of clothes in the storage unit I will have the perfect excuse to toss much of it into the thrift store bag. "If you haven't worn or used an item in a year, get rid of it." When I return it will be thirteen months since I packed it all away. Theoretically I could chuck it all based on that formula. There are a few things I look forward to wearing again and they're going straight into the closet. I have become accustomed to the limited choices in my closet, though I wish there was more variety. I went a little heavy on the stripes. My goal is to have a nearly empty closet and the freedom of choice that brings.

Departure looms ahead. I've scheduled a week in London for myself before heading home. My museum need will be met in a big way. In the meantime I'm packing, sorting, bagging, passing on what I cannot take. What I will take is many, many memories and a profound sadness at leaving this ancient land.

I will be packing home an oddly shaped vegetable peeler made in Turkey. I bought it in Albufeira, Portugal at the Oriente Perfeito. The condo we moved to after the cistern flooded in Boliquieme did not have a peeler, nor good knives. So I bought knives and, for less than two euros, the little coral colored peeler. It works well, but my reason for loving it is the Portuguese/Chinese/Turkish combo that it brings to mind every time I strip a carrot.

I think of Jacques Pepin and his instructions on how to use a knife to peel a vegetable. He pulls up toward himself, carefully positioning his fingers and wrist so that an errant pull doesn't slice him up. We Americans stroke the knife away from us so as not to cut ourselves. The Asian manner, so I'm told, and evidently the French manner, is to stroke the knife towards the self so as not to cut others. Individualistic society versus pluralistic societies. You see, I think deep thoughts while peeling veggies. Veggies, they're good for the body and the mind.

I'm deciding about packing a shirt I bought in Cork at TJ Maxx. I wanted a sleep shirt, couldn't find one that suited, and ended up in the clearance aisle where a long-sleeved Armani cotton T for 5 euros waited for me. Its inside tag said it had been made in 2014, though it doesn't say where, as US tags do. Wherever it came from I wondered about the path all the items we need or want take to get to us. Where had this shirt traveled since 2014 to land in the clearance aisle of the TJ Maxx in Cork, Ireland? What is the true cost of the shirt itself and all that travel? Still, it's soft and light, just right for a sleep shirt.

We had hoped that this trip would settle our ongoing question of where we want to live. Sonoma County is lovely, but we didn't return to Sonoma County because we loved it but because we loved our parents and wanted to take care of them as they aged. They are all gone now. Our children are grown and gone. We are, though too young for it, retired.

The ties that bind us are family ties. My brother, his wife, their daughter and her family, a nephew and his wife all live in Sonoma County. They are a reason to stay. My sister and her husband live in New Mexico. Husband's sister lives nowhere at the moment, in post-fire limbo waiting to see what comes next. She'll be with us for the interim.

Driving home today from dropping off some of husband's special chicken soup at a sick friend's home I remembered the two times I have felt truly at home. As newly marrieds we moved to Dana Point to a duplex on the hill above the harbor. The air, the ocean, the beach life made me so happy and peaceful that I felt a kind of relaxation, an 'at ease' feeling that felt like nothing before. I remember sitting on the steps enjoying the evening air and having a profound sense of being exactly where I should be, exactly where I wanted to be, of being home.

The place changed. We changed. We went from being a couple to a family of four. Orange County went from being a place where orange groves predominated to being the merge point of San Diego and Los Angeles. The freeways widened, the neighborhoods expanded, and the small-town era in southern Orange County was over.

Family circumstances brought us north again. It was a move of necessity, not a move home. We are glad to have been with family, helping family in those final years. I wouldn't change that for anything. Then the Great Recession of 2008 changed plans to move. Like so many people we couldn't afford to sell at the price we would have been offered. So we stayed. The inertia of having a job, friends, errands to do, weeds to pull, kept us in place. I used to say that home was where my family was. My husband, my children, our house. The kids are far away making their lives as they should, as we did at their ages. It's not loneliness that I'm feeling. It's a seeking for place, a knowing that I felt on those long-ago steps in the breeze.

A friend took a trip to Vienna more than thirty years ago. The bus ride from the airport into town settled the question for her. She was home. She returned to Orange County only to pack up and say goodbye to her parents. She has lived in Vienna ever since, perfectly at home.

A professor of mine experienced this phenomenon in a small town in France, not a touristy village, but a place where she felt immediately and completely home.

I felt at home in London. My navigational skills are better than ever now, but that bar has always been pretty low. When my sister and I traveled together she would use me for directions only when she was confused herself. This wasn't something that happened often as she, like our mother, seems always to know where she is, and which way is north. On the rare occasion when she got stuck she would ask me which way I thought we should go. Then she would go the opposite way, which was most often correct. Our first day in London coming up out of Victoria Station my sister was fumbling with the map to see which way to go to our B&B. I simply knew we needed to go left. I was right. Standing outside Victoria Station felt like coming home. My sense of direction was right on for the rest of the time in London. It's not a savant issue. I can't draw you a map of London, not even of its touristy highlights. Even when London doesn't make sense, as somewhere so ancient cannot do, it still feels right to me. I look forward to this solo week in London to see if the feeling persists. London too has grown like my first Dana Point home has. More people, more houses, more roads, more cars.

My separation anxiety has changed, maybe even lessened, during this year on the road. But it is still there. I forwarded a document to my husband "Kim's obit and instructions." It's my version of my life up to this point, reduced to a manageable size that will get the cheapest rate from the Press Democrat, plus a list of things I'd like to have done at the memorial. Any of you who have had to write an obituary know how much you would have liked details, dates, ideas, instructions on what to serve people after, music, location. Such a smart idea.

Husband says, "You're feeling anxious about going home."

"Yes," is all I can say because of the lump in my throat. It's not fear of flying. Separation anticipates death. That last glimpse at the Cork airport as I leave might be our last. The moment would be the same if I took the ferry to board a cruise ship to New York. One of us might not make it home. It's true. It's possible. It's not likely. Logic should dispel the anxiety, and it does for a few moments. When the sun is out and there are things to do it works. Then I find myself tearing up at the sight of one of the farm cats dashing through the yard again, or the hellebores opening their blooms and the daffodils I won't see in bloom pushing up their buds. I'm saying goodbye and it hurts. I was not so tearful leaving home as I am leaving Ireland. I knew I would return home to family and friends. But we might not return to Ireland as anything more than visitors.

"That was the last Monday night there," or "This is my last Tuesday doing this," and husband says, "Yes."

I'm grateful he doesn't try to talk me out of it. Let me swim in it awhile. Thirteen months of moving on, of packing up, of goodbyes, of leaving behind. I remind myself that there were, of necessity, in these thirteen months arrivals, hellos, making of friends, gathering, and learning. Departure leads to arrival.

We have been asked to speak for a few minutes to a group about what this last year has meant to us. It has turned my mind to the fullness of a year on the road, the fullness of traveling light, the openness to experience, to meeting new people, of learning something of other cultures, the peace of being outside our normal life. This way of thinking relaxes the anxiety. Still I ask husband to be sure he has saved my "obit" document somewhere he'll be able to find it easily. You can never be too sure.

I will miss the trails we have walked, the hills we have climbed, the views from which I have taken dozens and dozens of pictures, the crows, the cows, the sheep, the blue tits, the quick red fox, and the barn cats. I will miss the sweet, sharp scent of rain-drenched air. I will miss hearing the wind in the otherwise silent landscape. I will miss the lowing of the cows, and the generous slap of hard rainfall on the roof. I will miss walking into a shop and being known. I will miss a strong cup of Barry's Gold tea, the best in the land. Tears come thinking of the friends we have made and how far away they will be. I find I have gathered so many pleasant memories, made so many connections, that it is hard to think how we can leave. The first step towards home is London.

But first we have one last night in Cork.

Friends, three carloads, take us to a pub for music. We jostle around two small tables and perch at the bar by the table where the musicians are getting ready. Men with something like an accordion, drums, bagpipes, pipe, and a guitar are circling a small table lit by a candle set in a Jameson bottle. It is a grand evening of Guinness, beer, craik, music, and singing. I can't explain why, but I know there's something uniquely Irish about the fact that our night of fun was had in a pub next to the Jerh O'Connor funeral home. We take a group picture of that particular incongruity. I am reminded of another pub we enjoyed after playing at Myrtla Beach near Cork where we stepped over the slab laid outside the door inscribed "Still Stepping Over You Wesley." Is Wesley really under the slab?

For our last meal in Cork we walk down the street to what our friends say is the best fish and chips. It's a tiny place. Some of us end up outside in the soft Irish mist as it's so small. Rightly they said it's the best. The Fish Wife, if you ever get to Cork. I hope you do.

"What saves a man is to take a step. Then another step."

Henri Guillaumet, 1939, French aviator

London

It is an enormous, mesmerizing, energizing, amazing place that enlightens, inspires, annoys, and sometimes frightens me. The feeling of being home was not so profound this time as my other two visits, but still I felt more at peace in it than is right in a city of 8.1 million.

Others describe their reactions to London much more eloquently than I. What I feel is the history seeping up through the streets and exuding itself into the air. History that has been made, and history that is being made in the moment. I walk by Drury Lane of nursery rhyme fame. It is in old London, what the Romans called Londinium. The muffin man no longer has a shop there, but the street still exists, and not as a historical location roped off to tourists until the next group entry time. Zipping along in the bus I cross the old city gate sites, marked by columns topped with dragons. I drive by another arch that was put up for Queen Victoria. Go downstairs in the Guildhall Art Gallery and find the remnants of a Roman amphitheatre. They were digging down for a new building project and, whoops, there it was. Dig down in California and you find dirt.

Covent Garden has its roots in 7th century Anglo-Saxon history, and actually was a garden at one point. Now you share the history with all sorts of tourists, serious shoppers, and other wanderers. But to stand in a place and look up at the sky and think that people have been in this place for centuries, living out their lives fills me with joy. I have a sandwich and a chat with a Roman waiter at Maxwell's. He is unimpressed by 7th century origins, and since the restaurant we are in is only 300 years old, he shrugs. 'In Rome,' he tells me, 'the first century is young. You must go to Rome.'

Walking from Covent Garden I come across a store selling all a ballet dancer needs. Then there are art supply stores, and bookstores, Building is going on everywhere. History in the making in stone and glass as well as art and intellectual property at every turn. It's a relief to return to the hotel and find that Sipsmith gin is on special and they have Fever Tree tonic. I'm in for the night, thank you.

Hotels in London are notoriously expensive. Irish friends recommended the Premier Inns. Not expensive, not fancy, but clean and convenient, full breakfast included. I chose one kitty corner from the British Library, a place I intend to explore at length. My room looks over a commercial building and onto a neighborhood of homes. It turns out that dance classes are held in the building just below my window. Yoga, of course, one night. Women in saris and a man in leggings and a T-shirt another night. Modern dance another evening. I can sip my g&t and wish I was downstairs with the dancers.

One evening after enjoying the British Library I head out to meet friends. On the bus something hits the windshield. A snowflake the size of my hand, slushy and wet. I ask the bus driver if snow was expected. "Oh no," he says, surprised. It is a rare treat and potentially hazardous, but makes some great pictures falling against the lights of London. Back in Ireland, husband gets a larger snowfall. Mine is gone, turned to slush and rain by the time I go back outside that night. His lasts for a couple of days.

The next day is nothing but the British Museum. Like London it is huge, complicated, charming, frustrating, and worth all the effort. At lunch in the upstairs restaurant I look up to see a pair of feet behind a push broom on the glass roof. The waiter comes to place my soup in front of me and I ask him how often that happens. He looks up and in his accented English he says, "I've been here three months and it is the second time." Then he shrugs. Who knows the schedule of cleaners?

Closing time comes and I have done my best to see all that I could. Tired and sore footed I Google nearby restaurants and find Antalya only six minutes away. Beautiful ceilings, salty spicy perfect olives, very good Turkish food, excellent Port, attentive servers, and the melodious conversation of the two Turkish-speaking men at the next table make for a wonderful end to the day.

Many of the meals I have had in the past year were some combo of chicken, rice, vegetables, olives, wine. How many ways these basics can be made delicious and yet they are uniquely Portuguese, or Madeiran, or Irish, or Turkish.

The day I spend at the Tate Modern is misty and cool, a perfect winter day. As I approach the towers I find a large group of teens led by their teachers taking a while to walk diagonally across the forecourt. As they troop past, I see a dog running back and forth through their throng and around them. Then they pass and I see a man standing off at the left of the building. The dog runs to him, a ball is dropped, picked up by the man and tossed across the vast approach to the Tate. The dog is fast and a precise catcher. He rarely has to come more than halfway across the asphalt before he's mouthed the ball and returns to his master. I try to catch his acumen on video, but he's a tiny moving ball himself against the vastness of the Tate Modern. I contemplate what it would be like to live where I could think of the forecourt of a world class museum as a spot for a round of catch with the pets. It is this that I like about cities, the daily life in the midst of the urban rush, a neighborhood act in the midst of millions.

The Tate Modern is modern in both the best and worst sense of the word. It is a vast unwieldy building that formerly housed a power plant. Not built for beauty, its concrete solidity reeks of industrialism. Its lack of decoration speaks of the commercial 'Get it done' focus of such a building. Now it houses several floors of art. Pierre Bonnard "The Colour of Memory" was on exhibit while I was there. His nearly life size painting called "Summer 1917" sucked me in to its blue and green world that felt so like a delicious summer afternoon. The stroller-bound toddler accompanying his grandma insisted, as I did, on spending more time in front of it as well. A painter for all ages is our Pierre.

A bathtub nude evoked Klimt in blues and golds, but also imparts a hint of something unsettling. Perhaps it's the viewed-from-above perspective, or what might be an open window. In 1917 war was outside that window, a beautiful interior belying the horrifying exterior.

A piece on display echoed one of my favorite pieces at the De Young in San Francisco's Golden Gate Park: a wall hanging made of flattened bottle caps by Ghanaian artist El Anatsui called *Hovor II,* 2004. It turns out the Tate piece, *Ink Splash II*, 2012 is by the same artist. My taste is at least consistent.

Thank you, Google, for always having a "restaurant near me" on offer. That night it was the Tel Aviv-inspired dining experience of Bala Baya, which I found after a pleasantly rainy walk and a pause in a tunnel bathed in Tate blue.

The next day I got myself to The Garden Museum. It is a small place housed in a former church with no real garden except for the central court. In that central court is the tomb for Captain Bligh, a naval captain played by Anthony Hopkins in a movie loved by husband, *The Bounty*. I remind him via text that had he come to London he would have had a moment with a favorite moment of history. He is unimpressed and says he will watch the movie, again, instead. An ancient winding narrow stone staircase leads up to the roof where the views of London and the Thames are worth the claustrophobia and the exertion. Back inside, sponsored by Prince Charles, are displays of equipment, history, people (like Charlie Dimmock and Alan Titchmarsh of several BBC garden shows), and all things celebrating British gardens. I buy a pair of bright orange Deadheads to remember it by every time I snip spent flowers or errant stems from my plants. This stop is a refreshingly quirky highlight.

A quick lunch at the Riverside Café across the road and off to the Tate Britain. By now even I, lover of museums, am struggling with overwhelm. The morning of gardens and riverside and walking counterbalances the enormity of art and culture on offer. As I look back on my pictures, I realize how tired I was at this point. I took a few pictures of Tate's beautiful blue dome, and the intriguing black and white floor, and bought a card for a friend showing the photograph "Bird Gang" by Barbara Hepworth. I sat quite a while in the café nursing my tea as I contemplated a return to the galleries. I need to go back and do it all again.

I am near the Euston Street Station, a busy area of commuters and travelers via train, tube, bus, and taxi. When I return to Euston that evening, I find it packed with people staring up at the Arrivals/Departures board. Something has gone wrong somewhere and people mill around, shopping bags dangling, suitcases rolling behind, and the general murmur of voices rising and falling in question and story. It is lovely to not be one of the crowd. Out the door, up to the corner, and then left to the hotel for a g&t with a chicken skewer appetizer and monitoring of the dance class. Or, perhaps the British Library is open late and I can wander there, contemplating more history. Of course I love London! Her gifts are too numerous for such a short stay.

While sipping and snacking and watching I am also catching up on the newspaper and see the most endearing photo of a koala baby taking water from a bottle a man has offered him in the midst of Australia's latest heat wave. The kindness of humans.

The next day is back to the British Museum for two tours of Bible history items in the collections. When those are done, I think I will see what I missed when I spent a day there earlier in the week, but decide that I need air and light, so I take a bus, then walk to the Museum of London.

On my way I find a gate between two buildings leading to the Postmans Park. It was still light and only drizzling so I let myself into the garden. It widens out into a courtyard shared by several buildings. Artfully propped against the foundations are the headstones from the park's former life as a cemetery. Along one wall was a display of tiles telling the stories of various London heroes, the sort you don't usually read about. Children who saved other children from drowning, from fires, from horses' hooves or wagon wheels. Women who pulled others from burning buildings, only to succumb to smoke or flame themselves. Men who died saving family or workmates. And one for "William Fisher, aged 9, who lost his life on Rodney Road, Walworth, while trying to save his little brother from being run over. July 12, 1886." A few words to tell such a tragedy, and such heroics. As I read story after story I wonder how many descendants know their ancestors are memorialized on this wall at the side of the tiny Postmans Park on the way to the Museum of London. In my own search for relatives I find scraps of information that center on dates: birth, marriage, death, immigration, but only a few stories. I leave hoping that somewhere on someone's wall is a picture of young William or one of the other heroes, and that they tell the story to whoever will listen. "Yes, that's my great-great-grandmother. The night of the fire..."

Husband would have liked the garden and then the Museum of London. In the lobby is a wall describing Frost Fairs. "Between 1600 and 1814 it was not uncommon for the Thames to freeze over for up to two months at a time." This is followed by displays full of the stuff of human life pulled from the layers of London mud and dirt going back to the earliest settlements and coming forward to our time ending with a WWII bomb suspended overhead. After that depressing reminder of modern life it's off to Prezzo Pizza one block from my hotel and then the dance class for me.

Be advised there are only four good seats on a bus, the four up top in the front. Otherwise you're looking between people and over shoulders. I found this out on my last full day in London with a series of bus rides around the city, to Victoria Station, the Guildhall Museum, and finally to a glorious Lebanese meal at Maison Du Mezze that gives me the oomph needed to pack up for the next day's LHR to SFO flight home. Home. I'm still wondering what that is after all.

> "There are no foreign lands. It is the traveler only who is foreign."
>
> Robert Lewis Stevenson, Scottish novelist

Lessons

I wanted to be a good traveler. I did not want to be an Ugly American crashing my way through cultures. I wanted to be appreciative, grateful, and learn how to be something other than a spoiled Californian. We made some mistakes and stumbled across blessings through no expertise of ours. Time will tell how changed we are.

Practically speaking I wish I had packed the mini-binoculars, gotten International Driver's Licenses before leaving the US, as well as getting our medical histories on a Kaiser Medical flash drive – a service they provide. And, since our credit card provides auto insurance, but the Irish rental agency needed a letter stating that, I wish I had gotten the letter before we left.

I looked for this year on the road to show me where I wanted to live, and how to live simply. Where to live is still a question, partly because husband and I have different preferences and partly because as we have shifted into a different phase of life we are thinking of medical care and distance to doctors as well as beauty, solitude, proximity to a city. It's a hard mix to find.

Some things are simpler at home post-trip. My kitchen cupboards and drawers are emptier than before. The top shelves are empty. My implement drawer flies out at a tug because there is so little in it. My refrigerator is not cluttered with multiple varieties of salad dressings. My closet is less full. My shoe rack has open spaces. My linen closet is less packed. The garage is pared down to those things we actually use. My desk drawers are loose with roominess. Still, I cringe at the things we haven't let go of. Those cords and connectors, those files of something we may want someday, that old laptop that may have something on it that didn't get transferred, the Surface that I can't bear to part with even though I don't use it anymore, the files the law says I have to keep, and the trinkets of a lifetime.

After a year living from two suitcases and a carry on of electrical and medical gear it is hard to imagine we will actually need the abundance we still have. Without the impetus of a pending move or the deadline of a move to a storage unit it does not get moved out.

When I first returned, before husband was home, I unpacked my clothes and piled many of them into bags to go to the thrift store. Three more bags now sit in the garage ready to go. The pull to Macy's, Ross, Amazon, simply to buying is stronger here, perhaps because I know just where to go. Because I'm not thinking of how I'll fit it into a suitcase I'm more open to adding another skirt or dish or bathmat. I don't like it. Other than pulling the suitcases out and living out of them I'm not sure how to combat it.

When we have visitors in California we cringe anticipating they will want to go to the wineries. They are world class, but we drive by them multiple times a week and have become inured to them. My lesson for home is to be grateful, to live with eyes open, and an appreciative heart, to gladly share my heritage with our visiting friends. I am fourth-generation Californian. My great-grandparents are buried in Sebastopol. My family tree is littered with Sonoma County locations. Husband is first-generation Californian, born in San Francisco, raised in Paradise and Sonoma. I do not want to be complacent about my history, to be unimpressed with the bounty of our abundant heritage.

Memorial Day

We have things to remember, people to mourn. This year we are dealing with husband's recovery from a long-avoided surgery. He received a diagnosis of cancer nine years ago. It was the sort that could be watched, the sort that did not require an immediate trip down Cancer Hell Lane. But when we returned and made our rounds of doctors and dentists his numbers had changed, and he decided it was time.

Plans to return to Ireland after helping his sister get settled in Paradise are out. Helping his sister is now very limited. Paradise itself is very limited. Its recovery, unlike Santa Rosa's, will be longer, harder, and possibly unsustainable. Husband's recovery will be long and hard also.

Our trips to Kaiser mean going over Fountain Grove Parkway where the Tubbs fire ravaged neighborhood after neighborhood, where my son's in-laws ran for their lives along with all the others, including Dr J and Ms S who lived across the road from them. Each time we make the run there is a combination of memories of the fire, revulsion for the loss, and absolute disbelief that people are rebuilding wood framed homes in the path of the next fire. Granted, there are tile and metal roofing, the siding is now the cement fiberboard that reduces flammability, but probably not in an inferno like the Tubbs fire. The ubiquitous wood fences stretch between houses like a fuse waiting to be lit.

What we did notice when we first had to drive over the hill before we left for our year on the road was that the city buildings mostly survived. Single story, cement block walls, metal roofs, and few windows. Yet people are rebuilding wood framed two-story homes on ridges despite what they know.

Except for husband's former boss. He and his cul-de-sac neighbors lost their homes that night. He is rebuilding the homes with cement walls and other fire-resistant techniques. He shares my wonder at the return to the building style that allowed homes to be incinerated within minutes.

We built a home in 2001 out Highway 128 near Cloverdale. We were far enough from the nearest fire station that we had to meet a number of criteria to qualify for reasonable fire insurance, and to meet the requirements for the fire department to be happy to respond. We sided the house with cement fiberboard, roofed it in metal, circled it with a composite, less flammable decking product, surrounded the house with a 30′ wide ¾" gravel bed, installed a 2,500 gallon water tank for the exclusive use of the fire department, and set hoses and sprinklers around the property. We kept the front pasture mowed and trimmed the trees. Our property had redwoods on one side, a year-round creek, and oak woodland running up the hill behind us. We received the best possible insurance rate and the approval of the fire department. I think it would burn as fast as any of those that went the night of the Tubbs inferno.

When we were looking to move from that country house to something closer to my now widower dad and to my new job, I drove my father around with me looking at properties. He was mid-stage Alzheimer's at the time and often not sure where he was. One day I drove him to Los Alamos Road, a narrow winding road up a mountain, to look at a house for sale. In one of the moments of clarity that come to many Alzheimer's patients my dad asked what we were doing on this road, one he knew well himself.

"There's a house for sale somewhere."

"Kid," he said, "if there's ever a fire up here you'll never get out alive."

I stopped the car in the middle of the road and began a multi-point turn. By the time we were facing downhill Dad was lost in the Alzheimer's again, carefully sipping his coffee.

The wisdom of a California native. Pass it on. And travel light.

Acknowledgements

There are so many without whom we could not have done these thirteen months on the road. First, Chet and Cyd, Kris and Gerry, and Bart and Lynda for saying "Go! Do it!" when we called them about the bizarre offer to rent. Then my brother and sister-in-law, Chet and Cyd, who said, 'Sure, come stay with us for the few days until the tenants are settled in.' Then we all got the horrible flu that was going around that January and were down for about ten days. We boomeranged back to their home as we scooted off to various family members and friends, until the day my sister-in-law drove us to San Francisco International for our flight to Portugal, probably to make sure we were really gone this time.

Then they took care of picking up our mail and generally acting as our agents for the Irish Immigration needs. She also got our ATM replacement card to us via snail mail, despite the fears of Mary Anne and Symon at Chase bank.

I would like to list all the friends we made in Albufeira, Madeira, Fermoy, and Nenagh. That would be too much, so I'll name just a few.

In Albufeira: Nici, Seeu and Eija, Mick and Bronwen, Jerry and Sarah.

In Funchal: João and Tracy, Linda, Tiago, Frank and Lorraine, Richard and Karen.

In Fermoy: Mike, Thomas, Mike and Lynn, Danny and Sarah, Richard and Jenny, Pauline, Gen, Ken and Mary, Martin and Margaret, Martin and Lisa, Jessie, Shannon, Brian and Sonia and family, Ross and Esther and family, Max and Susanne, Danilo and Priscilla, Kevin and Kassia, Sascha and Danielle and Oliver and Lena, Josh and Abby and Bethany, Caleb, and Jared, Patrick, Jonathan and Anna, Jim and Rebecca, Claomar, Jennifer, Cesar and Edileia.

And finally, in Fermoy a special mention of the delightful family we met in Albufeira, Portugal who got us a house in Fermoy, Ireland: Peter, Christine, and David.

In Nenagh: Steve and Diane (who connected us to castle and car), John and family, Merrill and Esther, Tim and Cara, Chelsea, David and Millie.

There are more, I know. I apologize to those who I've inadvertently left out. My heart is full of happiness from the privilege of getting to know you all and experiencing your kindness and love. May husband and I pay it forward in a manner worthy of you.

Epilogue

October 2019 brought another series of fires to California. Our particular monster was the Kincade. PG&E executed a new strategy of planned power outages to prevent their equipment from starting fires. At this point no one is sure what started the Kincade beast, but PG&E did report a power system issue about four minutes before the first report of fire at the scene of the power system issue.

It seems certain that there would have been more fires if PG&E hadn't cut power to thousands. We were eleven days without power through five separate outages. The final outage was not PG&E's fault. A drunk driver missed a turn on our road, flipped his truck into the creek, and started two fires. The winds were mild and the emergency response swift. The fires were put out, the drunk man taken away to jail. Eight hours later we had power again.

Our firefighters in California are the best in the world. The lessons learned in 2017 led to a whole new approach to fires. In 2019 firefighters were out and around the county ready to start fighting. Residents were evacuated early so firefighters could be firefighters, not rescuers. It made a tremendous difference. "Only" 174 homes lost.

The 2020 Glass Fire put us on the road again, but only as far as San Jose. Now we are home again waiting for the evacuation warnings to be lifted and I am sure I hear the road calling.

Travel Hacks

Nothing here you won't have read before, but these things make travel easier for me.

Two checklists follow in the next pages: one for a Go! emergency and one for basic travel planning.

Less is better. Whatever you're doing and wherever you're going, this is true. Unless you are going to deepest, most isolated Africa or the Amazon, you can probably buy what you need if you went too far in eliminating things from your suitcase.

Scout out small containers to use in your toiletries. For instance, a plastic tube that once held mini-M&Ms makes a perfect Q-tip holder. Buy the travel size of your favorite shampoo and conditioner and save them for refills. Use liquid soap; bars are too messy. Use a lipstick as blush because the container is smaller. Aveda makes eyeshadow that comes in a tiny holder that can accommodate two shades and lasts a long time. Find a salon near you.

A couple of bulldog or binder clips can do many things: hold a skimpy towel closed; clip together those too-small curtains; hold papers and passport securely. You'll come up with your own list.

Layer.

Label stuff. When you are jet lagged in a poorly lit hotel room you'll be glad.

Bring spares of things you can't replace without a doctor's prescription, like glasses, contact lenses, copies of prescriptions.

Different sizes of Ziplocks. Think of wet swimsuits, washcloths, etc.

A washcloth or two if you use them because they are not always provided in Europe.

A micro-terry towel just for your hair if you use them because see above.

Read *"The Travel Skills Handbook"* by Rick Steves of Europe Through the Back Door. If you're going to museums read his *"Europe 101 History and Art for the Traveler"* and *"Mona Winks: Self-Guided Tours of Europe's Top Museums"*.

When ticketing I follow, or try to follow, the advice of Nomadic Matt (nomadicmatt.com): don't spend more than an hour looking for a deal. Just book it. Your time and sanity are worth more than what you might, maybe, could save by scouring another site or waiting to see if prices go down, which they probably won't. Use several consolidators to see what's out there. Then choose an airline or two you would like to fly on. Go to their sites. If there's a problem later with your ticket it will be easier to get help from the airline itself. If you use the consolidator, you have to work through them, and that can get complicated.

Unless you really like takeoffs and landings, don't book a multi-stop ticket. Get to your destination as easily as you can. A direct flight can be well worth the price difference in saved time, and wear and tear on you.

Have fun with the house hunting/hotel selecting process. It will be your home away from home. Balance the money with the experience. But remember, you will be asleep for a third of your time at your destination. So, maybe save some money to spend on the experience.

Indulge in traveling like a local. Use the bus, tube, subway, metro, tram, boat, or train. Rent a car only in those places where you need to get somewhere those public modes of transport don't go. Traveling with locals will be some of the best times on your trip.

If a local invites you somewhere, go.

Finally, put away all your expectations and journey on.

GO!

With 5 mins notice	10 mins notice	1 hour + notice	2 hours + notice
keys	jewelry clothes	food	
wallet	papers, et al	stuff	
phone, tablet	Emergency stuff		

Go! bag

Papers, et al	self	mate	Location	Clothes:	self	mate	Location
Home/Auto ins				underwear			
DMV info				pants / shorts			
Med hx				t-shirts / tops			
laptop				shoes / tennies			
flash drives				swimsuits / cover			
Passport(s)				pajamas			
Vet info				sweater(s)			
				jacket(s)			
				sweats			
Emergency!				**Stuff:**			
Money				bathroom stuff			
chargers/batteries				daypack			
flashlights				blowup mattress			
Meds				laundry bag			
radio							

Packing List

CLOTHES:	self	mate	child	STUFF:	self	mate
underwear				bathroom stuff		
				makeup		
swimsuit / cover				blow dryer		
t-shirts				jewelry		
shorts						
				tablet(s)		
pants				books/mags		
blouses						
shoes/ tennies				journal		
				daypack		
suit / ties				maps/guidebooks		
shirts						
skirts				planner		
dresses				chargers		
				TICKETS!		
nighties				MONEY!		
sweats				dirty clothes bag		
				wet clothes bag		
sweater(s)						
jacket(s)				food / cooler		
				water / snacks		
WINTER:						
snow gear				binocs		
				loupe		
SUMMER:						
pool floats						
chair / umbrella						
sleeping bag(s)						
air pump						
beach bag						
sunscreen						

What I packed:

2 coats (one a fold-up-into-a-pocket raincoat)
2 sweaters
14 shirts (summer + winter)
3 scarves, lightweight
5 skirts
3 pair pants
4 pair shoes (sandals, tennies, dressy walkers, flip flops)
2 pair pajamas
Workout clothes – 2 sets

What I bought:

Replaced the dressy walkers I wore out on Portuguese cobblestones.
One dressy shirt in Fermoy just because.
Two t-shirts, one Portuguese and one Irish, for work outs.
1 sleep shirt.
1 fringed sweater because: fringe.
2 scarves because I didn't pack turtlenecks and an Irish winter is cold.
1 pair ankle boots for the reason noted above.
1 sun hat in Albufeira, Portugal
1 sun hat in Funchal, Madeira
1 sun hat in Mitchelstown, County Cork, Ireland

What I left behind:

3 shirts
1 sweater
1 skirt
Ankle boots
Dressy walkers
1 sun hat in Albufeira, Portugal
1 sun hat in Funchal, Madeira
1 sun hat in Fermoy, County Cork, Ireland

About the Author

Kim McGrath is a fourth-generation Californian. She is a Licensed Marriage and Family Therapist and a Licensed Professional Clinical Counselor currently living, once again, in Santa Rosa, California with her husband, Bob.